CLOSET CASES

QUEERS ON WHAT WE WEAR

MEGAN VOLPERT

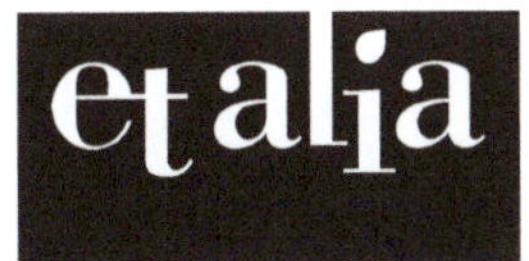

etaliapress.com
Little Rock, Arkansas
2020

sartorial: relating to tailoring, clothes, or style of dress

satori: sudden enlightenment

This book is dedicated to queers in closets everywhere.

Our boots have blood on them. Our struggle to find the perfect shirt is real. Our conflicting feelings about the color pink are valid. May our bodies not feel like emergencies. May our clothes not shrink in the wash. May the fierceness of these contributors help us all to open the closet door and step into a more fabulous future.

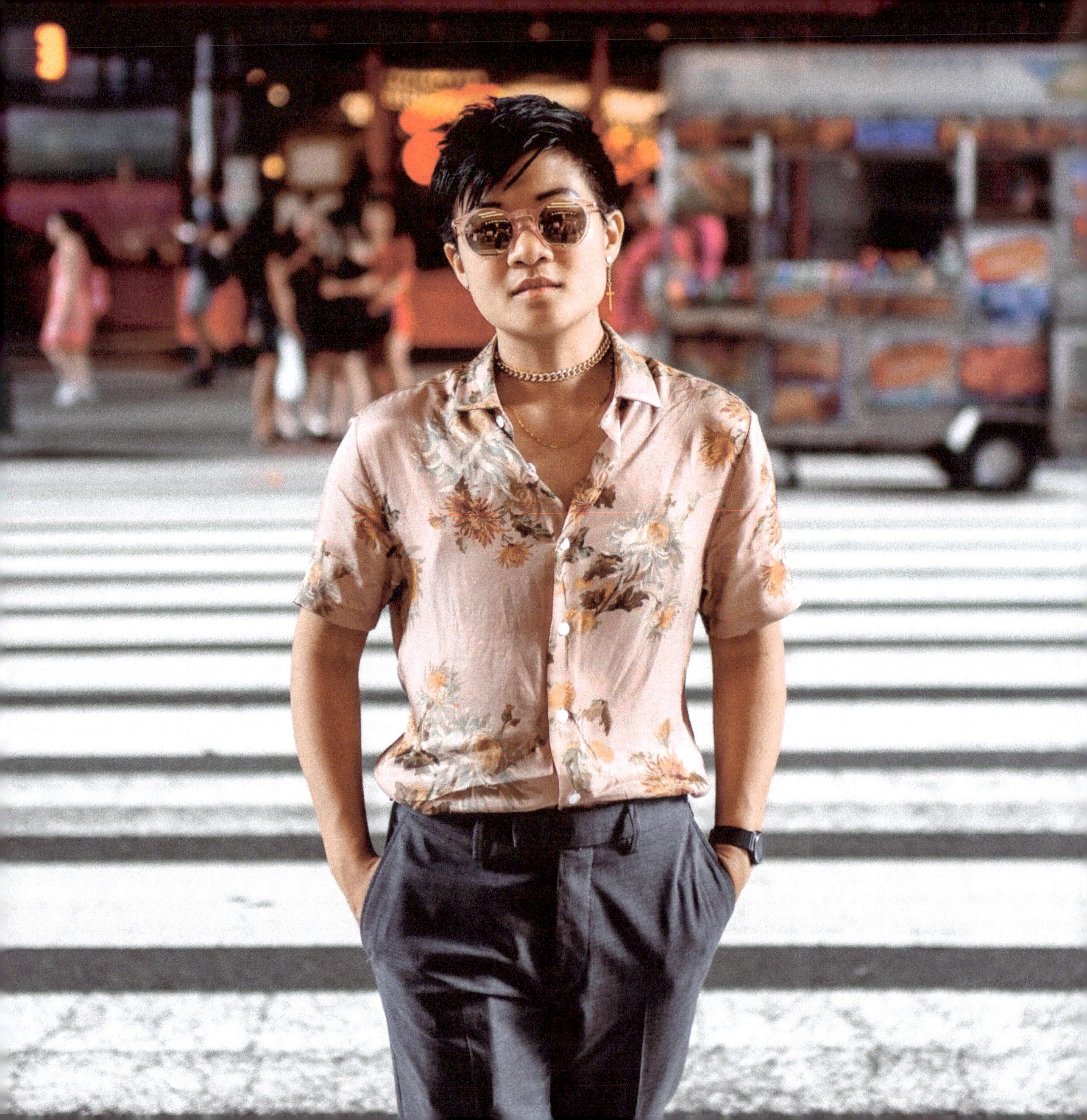

SUMMER OUTING

my mom told me to wear more pink
more jewelry: jīn;
to pray more to jesus
m o r e—
so i sent her this photo;
[Read 3:16pm]
[Read Yesterday 3:16pm]
[Read 07/04/18 3:16pm]

--

pink, jīn, jesus, jender
i am m o r e of everything
and enough for me.

AIRIN YUNG is a queer, trans, non-binary individual passionate about diversifying the practice of law. Though their career is focused on health law and policy in Washington, D.C., they are, at heart, a musician and performer from the San Francisco Bay Area.

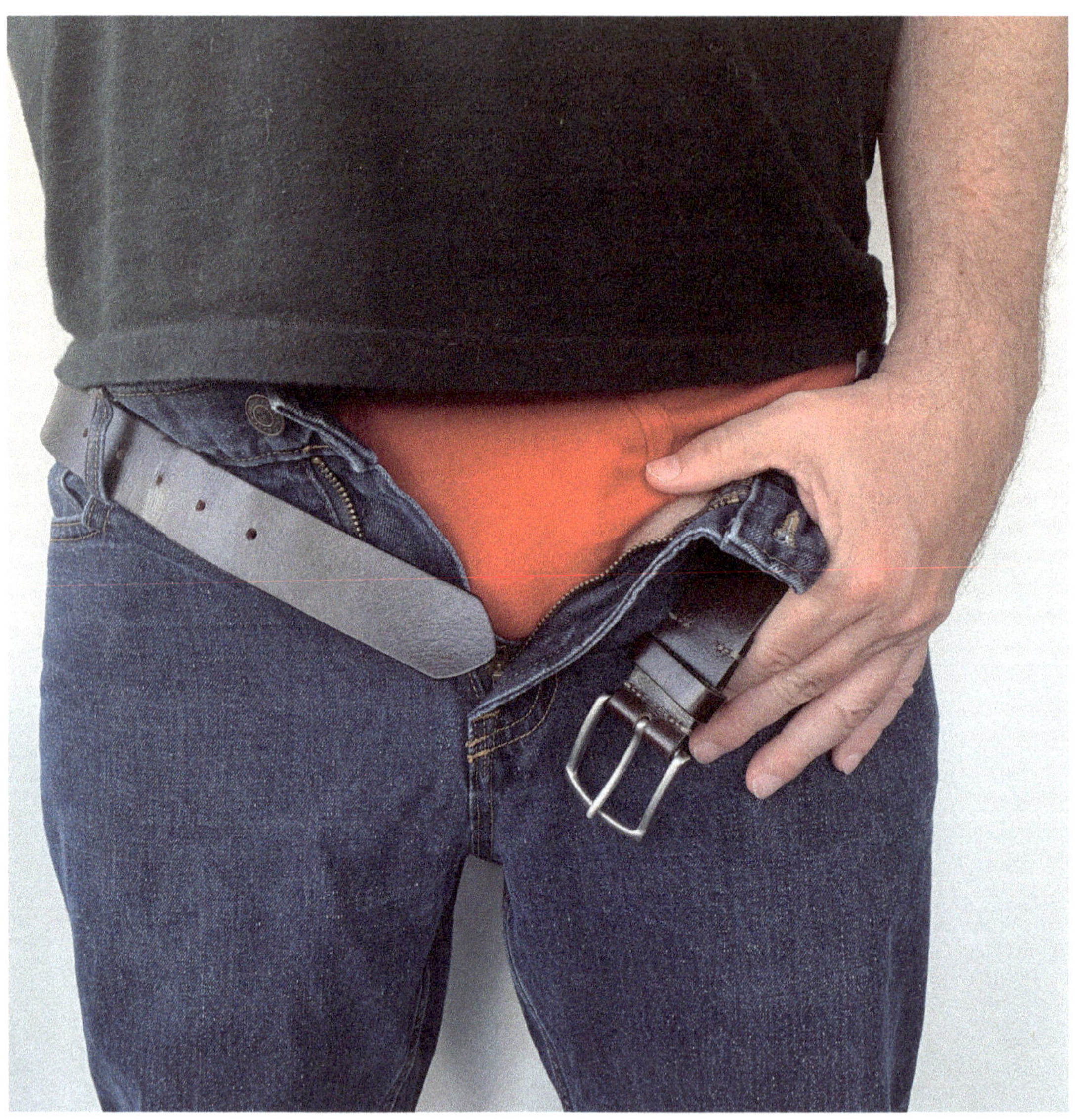

GERARD WOZEK is the author of *Dervish*, which won the Gival Press Poetry Award. His book, *Postcards From Heartthrob Town*, is a collection of short travel stories selected for the Haworth Press "Out in the World" Travel Literature Series. He is currently at work on a memoir about being adopted.

A BRIEF HISTORY OF MY UNDERWEAR

My mother believed in the power of bleach.

For all the years I was growing up, she was keen on meticulously separating the whites from the colored clothing and soaking the cotton undershirts and underwear in a lukewarm mixture of Borax and baking soda. Her constant search for store-bought whitening elements, from Blue Borateem to "double-action" Biz, made her a sort of alchemist, a mad scientist searching to make every undergarment as sanitized and blanched as possible.

But it was her relentless devotion to having her son wear the whitest boy briefs that drove me to a kind of emotional trauma.

"If you should get into an accident one day and they have to take you to the hospital," she would warn me, "I want to make sure you have the cleanest, whitest briefs on when they begin to undress you."

Terrified that I would one day "soil" my undergarments, I took great pains to make sure I was always wearing clean undies. The "tight-ie whities" as my brother referred to them, had to be spotless in both the crotch and seat, and heaven forbid, absent any signs of faded graying or dullness.

Every holiday, from birthday to Christmas, it was always the same, an economy selection of six Fruit of the Loom traditional boy briefs, neatly gift wrapped and offered to me with the same superior-sounding adage, "You can never have too many 'whities,' right?"

I tried to answer my mother with a smile as I secretly lusted for tropical printed Hawaiian bikini-style shorts. Or neon orange and yellow thigh-rise briefs. Or multi-colored striped boxers, or low risers with a brightly embroidered monogram. Later on, in my junior year of high school, I dreamt of soft California madras against my loins, or handsewn undershorts made of genuine India silk. Anything but the ordinary bleached-white briefs I felt relegated to wear.

At seventeen, my attention shifted to men's underwear ads for release. I'd imagine myself playful with the athletic models sitting out poolside on lounge chairs who just happened to be wearing tight-fitting, shape-showing green paisley boxers. Or laughing with the underdressed guys at the basketball court who fit snugly into their animal print high-rise Jockeys and tartan plaid bulge-enhancing pouchies.

After a rebellious short period of going commando, I wound up leaving home at eighteen and embracing my own queer-identified obsession with men's underwear: everything from pink satin jock cups to leather and lace sissy pouch panties. I'd laugh back then, imagining the paramedic who would treat a proud gay man wearing see-through purple mesh bikinis.

Now in my mid-life, I have become, again, more conservative in my undergarments. Gone are the wilder days of sheer g-strings and slinky thongs or "gay boy" branded undies like Joe Snyder or Hom; instead, I've returned to a simple, retro low-waisted brief. Colors, though, stay in. No one will ever find bleach in my laundry basket. I prefer to wear the rainbow.

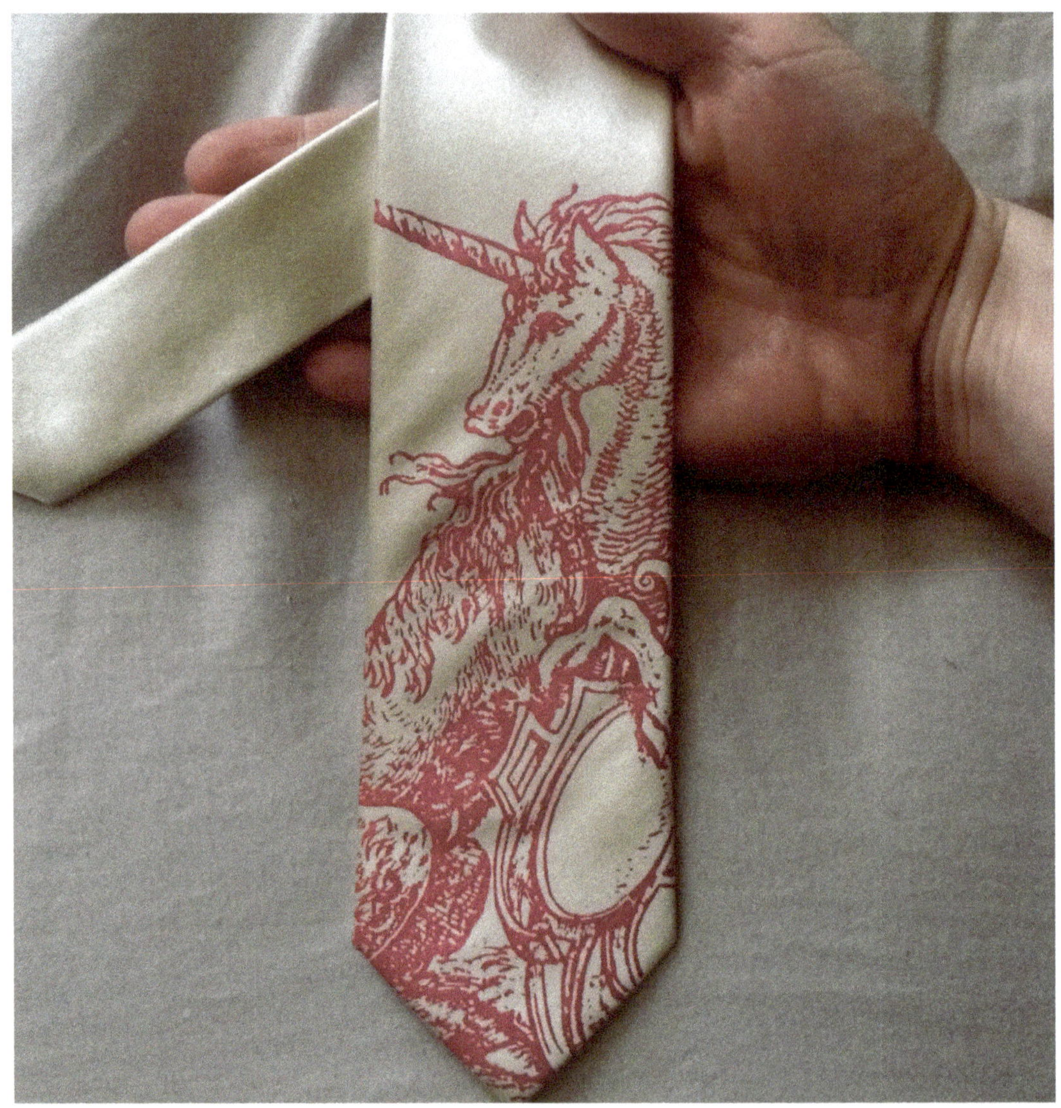

LUCAS WILDNER is a poet, essayist, and teacher in southern King County, Washington. His current project examines the relationships between internalized homophobia and white privilege. Recent and forthcoming work lives at *Night Music Journal, Honey and Lime, Nice Cage, birds piled loosely,* and elsewhere.

BIND

This started because I didn't want the hall monitors to ask me for my pass again. An incident after filling out paperwork that triggered imposter syndrome about my first school year. Until the final traces of boyhood burned away, leaving a white-collar professional in his wake, I would wear a tie to school. Every day.

The effects were widespread. I earned Sirs in the cereal aisle after work and polite handshakes from parents at conferences.

Was I attempting to pass as straight? I took advantage of a legible masculinity: once, students played matchmaker, discussing which of the three single women in the faculty I would be most compatible with. Success!

Yes, I hated myself. Worse, I feared being fired if I came out—an internalized homophobia that equated gays with pedophiles.

In class, we'd discuss how a speaker needed to set up a persona to engage their audience—to share belief in common values. I had reached for easy symbolism, a hetero-patriarchal costume. Anyone could walk in and find the teacher in seconds.

A baby gay, I hadn't yet examined why I felt normative masculinity was the prerequisite for respectability, for good teaching. Mr. Wildner was straight, cis, white. Safe.

Thankfully, the internet broke him. My poems—often glittery—began to float up to the surface whenever bored students typed in my name. A few reached out in appreciation. The haters—fearing an F or whatever other ludicrous punishment I would mete out—stayed quiet, or complained to administration, who did not bother to pass along their concerns. I got lucky.

In year three, I gave myself permission to buy a gay tie—cream with a hot pink unicorn. Not the subtlest choice, but liberation fills self-loathing's vacuum. It was a step toward queering my understanding of tricky pedagogical concepts—what allows different students to trust and respect a teacher? What ideas about adulthood/masculinity/sexuality was I modeling?

A master's tool with a half-Windsor knot is still a master's tool. These days, in my *Magneto was right* era, I wish I had bought a dress.

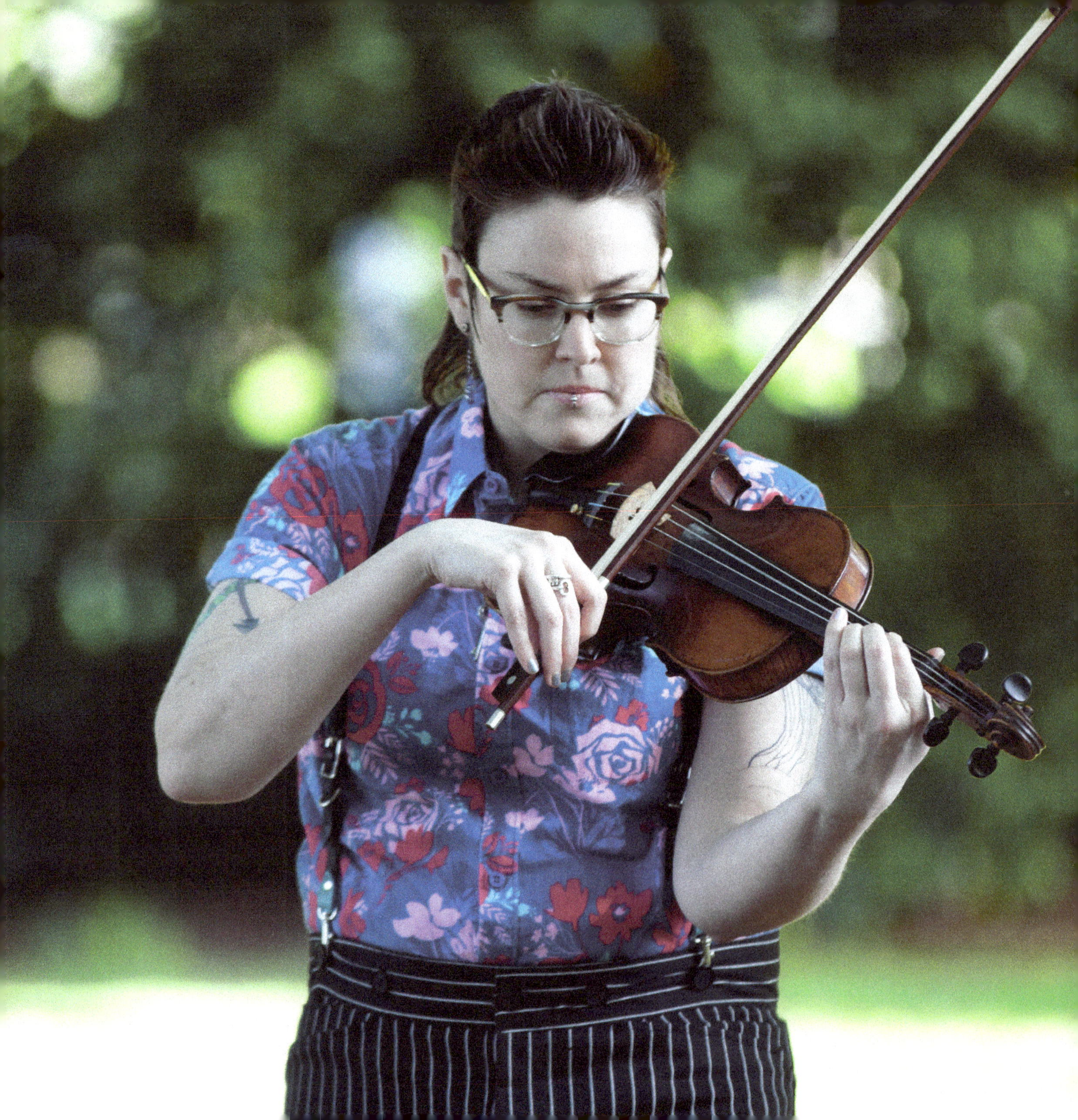

MY GENDER IS

Matching nail polish and bow tie
Power tool for jewelry making
Boyband choreography at sunset
Turquoise glitter eyebrows
Pinstripes and floral print
Suit vest under denim vest
Single earring on whichever side is the gayest
Suspenders worn like a harness
Ferns and passion flowers
Fae time traveler
Daddy in a skirt
Trinity knot and other fancy twists
Gold sequin high-waisted shorts with a bulge
Plaid on plaid on plaid
Backpack and newsies cap
Being mistaken for a 16-year-old boy by the
    small-town librarian
Houndstooth pants and purple hiking boots
Electric violin curled against my shoulder
Dyke Faggot Genderqueer
Stripy fingerless gloves
Flannel giraffe sheets
Banjolele strung on a rainbow
Spaceships and dinosaurs

90s Nickelodeon sweatpants
Tie clips and red slips
Flagging with fruit fabric to an interview for
    a fruit tree pruning company
Magenta wool fedora, cocky and cocked
Dapper dandy non-profit professional
Magical changeling
Lightning bolts and boner jokes
Writing a sci-fi musical about unicorns and
    capitalism
Well-earned silver glitter in hair flip and tails
Playroom of costumes and mirrors
Selfies for days
Coveralls on the weekends
Summer of mesh
Flogography and flowcharts
Infinity scarf made of recycled sweaters
Sandcastles decorated with wood, stone, shell,
    and feathers
Eyeliner and glitter beards
Aqua-lined suit from a production of *The Music
    Man*
Dandelion growing out of gravel

MAX VOLTAGE is a Portland-based genderqueer musician, writer, performer, choreographer, playwright, and producer. Max's queer camp artist sensibilities and radical politics were forged in the world of drag, but their fascination with gender, costumes, and performance has been lifelong. Max is the creator of *Reclaiming Pink*, a one-homo-show about gender; *Homomentum*, a satirical post-earth sci-fi musical; and *Turnback Boyz*, a time-traveling queer boyband, where they play Peter Pansy, a glam-dandy fiddler from the future. Max is a classically trained violinist and uses a loop station to compose and perform as a solo artist and with their band Sparkle & Truth.

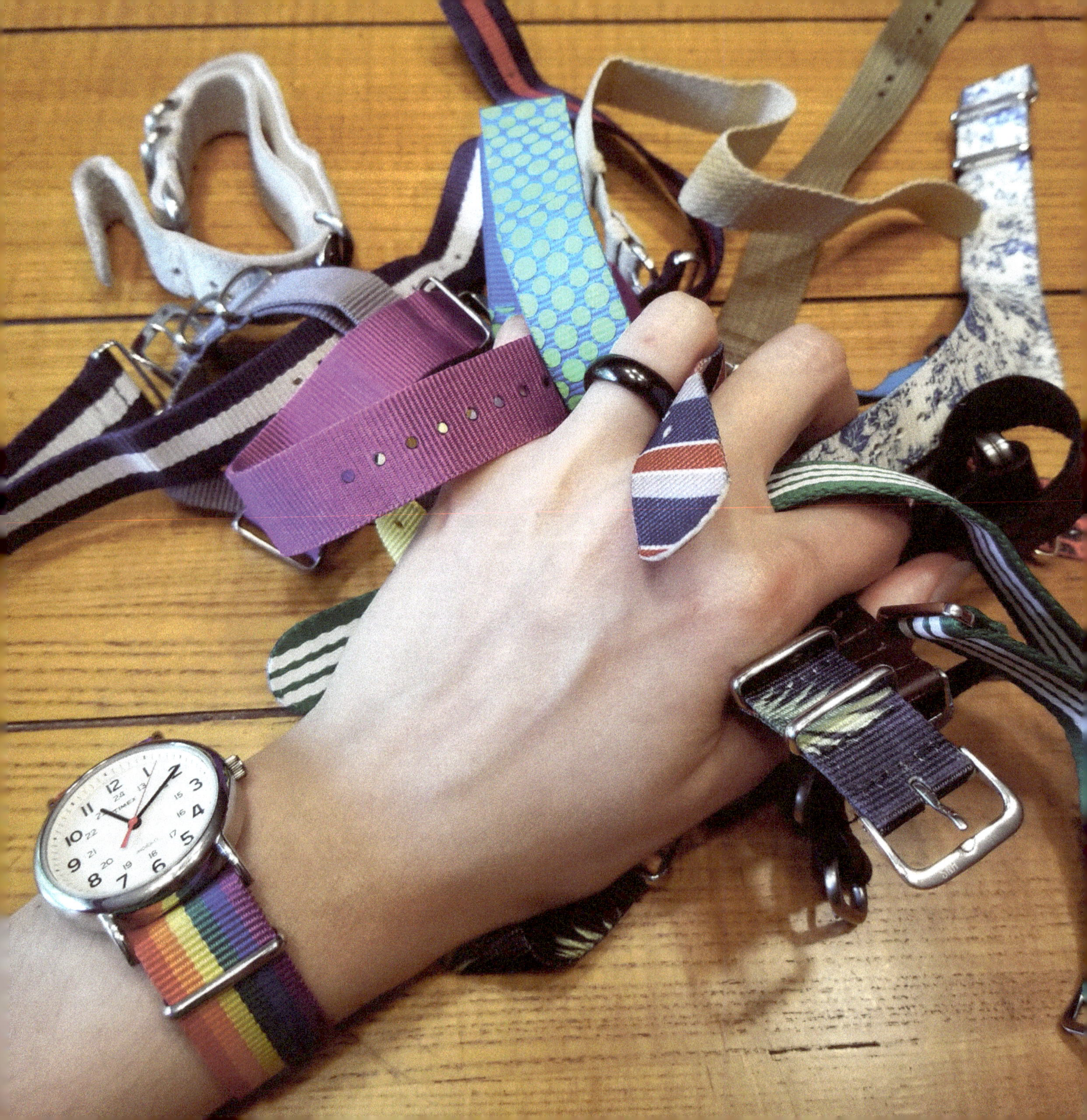

WATCHDOG

Time is against us is how most queers feel. We're always waiting for the other shoe. Even watching a polite and tidy sitcom like *Will and Grace*, I catch myself thinking Jack's going to get the shit beat out of him any day now. Or AIDS, or jail, or homelessness. I have two openly queer friends who work in high schools like I do. They both retired this year. The way we counted those days down you'd think we were in NYC for NYE 1999. If you're queer and you finish out your career by natural means instead of getting fired, that's living the dream.

The Timex Weekender is a cheap dial that makes a big sound. Tick tick tick. All the time. Time was coming hard for me and I started running. Worked faster. Thought faster. Stopped for no one. Accomplishments as far as the eye could see. This ten-dollar watch ran me. I couldn't stand it and gave the watch away a few days after I put it on, by which time it had aged me several months. A lot of other things happened over many more moons and I survived them all. The person I am now meditates about twenty minutes a day. Every day, tapping the ancestors.

You know what they say? Tick tick tick. How precious it is to finally respect a few of one's elders. How invigorating to have lasted one more minute in this queer body in this strange life. How brave to simply keep showing up and how aggravating for the other bastards that one's accomplishments keep aggregating. Also accumulating are a diverse bunch of watch bands, because I ponied up another ten bucks to reclaim my Timex. The person I am now happily straps on this constant reminder to hold steady.

Sometimes in a contentious meeting my admin will sit back in his chair and I can almost see him calculating whether this is the hill I die on. It never has been so far. And while he's thinking about it in the hostile silence of the conference room, I'm telegraphing him that queer agenda: tick tick tick.

MEGAN VOLPERT is proud to have edited this anthology. She is the author of many books on popular culture, including two Lambda Literary Award finalists, a Georgia Author of the Year finalist, and an American Library Association honoree. Her newest work is *Boss Broad* (Sibling Rivalry Press, 2019). She has been teaching high school English in Atlanta for over a decade and was 2014 Teacher of the Year. She writes for *PopMatters* and has edited anthologies of philosophical essays on the music of Tom Petty and the television series *RuPaul's Drag Race*.

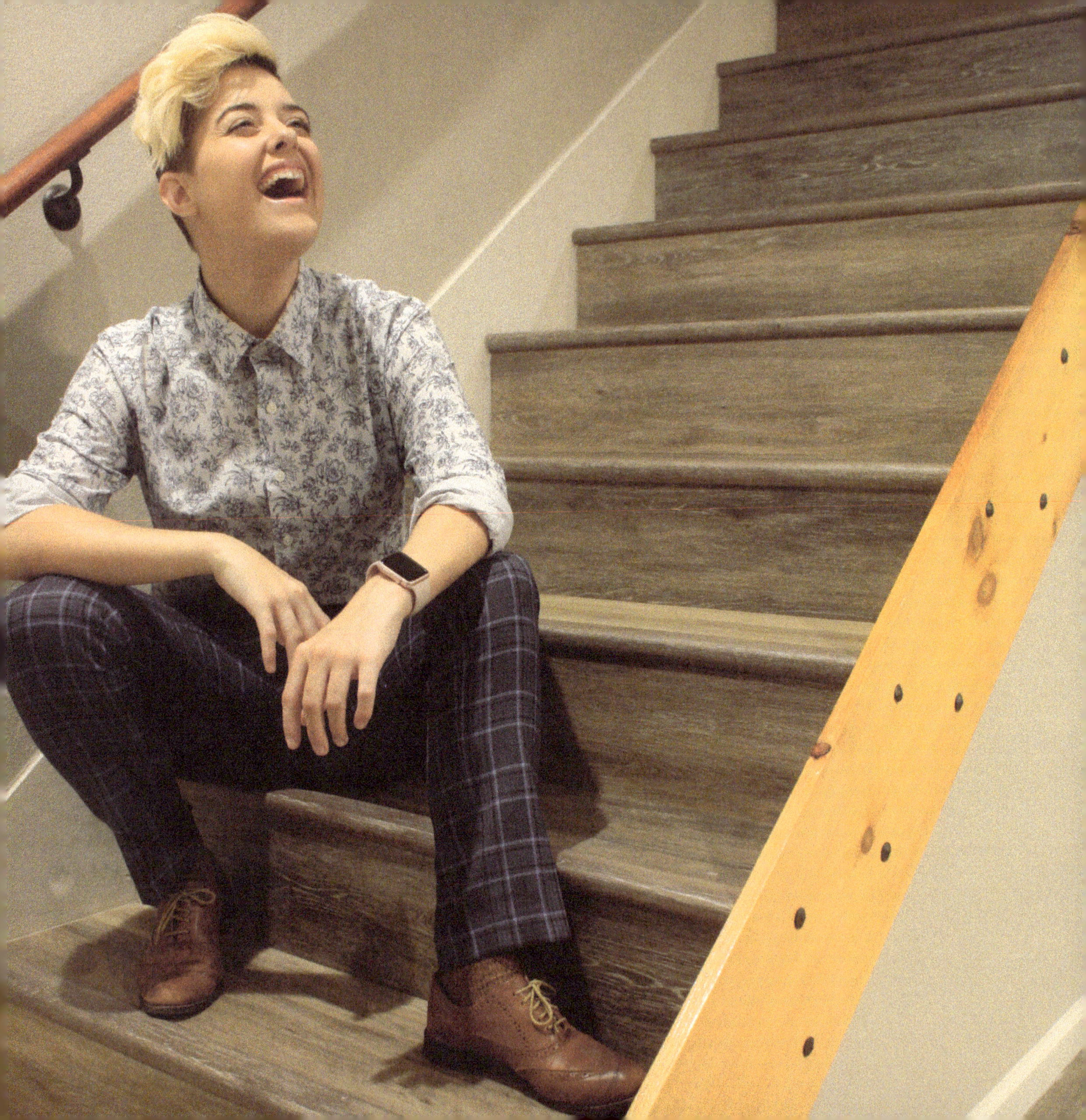

BLUSH AND BUTTON DOWN

There's something about putting our face on
gets us eyes wide, flush with alive

Something about flowers on our button down
makes us feel
                        rebellious.

Clash pattern,
          gender-bent twist

we are we   loud and lovely   power and
pretty

There's something about break / ing boundaries

We never did well with them anyway

finds us unquestionably
                                  queer.

These classics

get us   dancing

AL VANSICKLE is a 21-year-old creative
writing student at the University of Central
Arkansas who writes poetry and fiction.

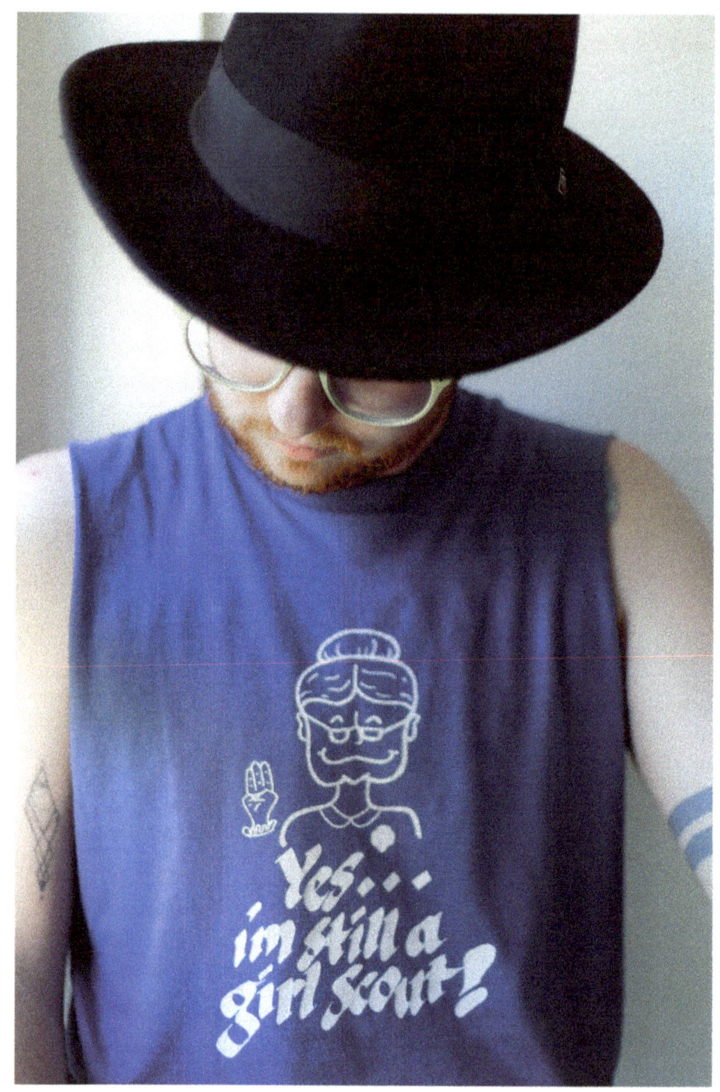

PARRISH TURNER is a queer essayist and editor who hails from Georgia. His writing focuses on gender, sexuality, spirituality, regionality, and more. Turner's work has been featured on *Buzzfeed*, *Slate*, *Culture Trip*, *Gertrude Press*, and *The Rumpus*. With his fellow playwrights, he was honored with the Metro Atlanta Theater award for his work on the musical *By Wheel and By Wing*. Turner was a 2014 Lambda Literary Fellow and received his MFA from The New School in 2017. He is currently working as a freelancer based in Brooklyn and is always on the lookout for a great cup of tea. Photo by Juno Rosenhaus.

YES . . . I'M STILL A GIRL SCOUT

My best clothes come to me. I rarely shop for clothing and usually have an eye more for utility than style. But when something finds its way into my possession, I know it is serious. So when my roommate Jourdan burst into my room, excited from her thrifting trip, I was open.

"We found the perfect shirt for you. Well, it was between this and a yellow shirt with a cursive 'butch,' but we were on the fence about that one," she blurted as she pulled out a shapeless and worn blue t-shirt. *Yes . . . I'm still a girl scout!* the shirt read with a cartoon elderly woman.

It only took a few years on testosterone for people to begin looking surprised when I mentioned that I was transgender. Reactions ranged from utter shock to concern about any help I might need on this upcoming change, apparently forgetting that people go the "other" direction. While affirming, I felt something disappearing as I began to blend in.

I am either a member of the Scouts or the Girl Scouts, depending on who I talk to and how much I want them to know. I was a Girl Scout for 12 years, earning my Gold Award (significantly more difficult than the Eagle Scout Award), and was gifted a lifetime membership to the Girl Scouts of America for my efforts. This huge part of my life must be glossed over or navigated deftly, lest I misrepresent my current self to those not able to handle nuance.

But this t-shirt was the answer to my prayers. I lopped the sleeves off and found myself wearing the tank everywhere. It is a wink and a smile to those who bother to read it and a nod to those who pick up on its layers of meaning. Plus, it makes me feel sexy.

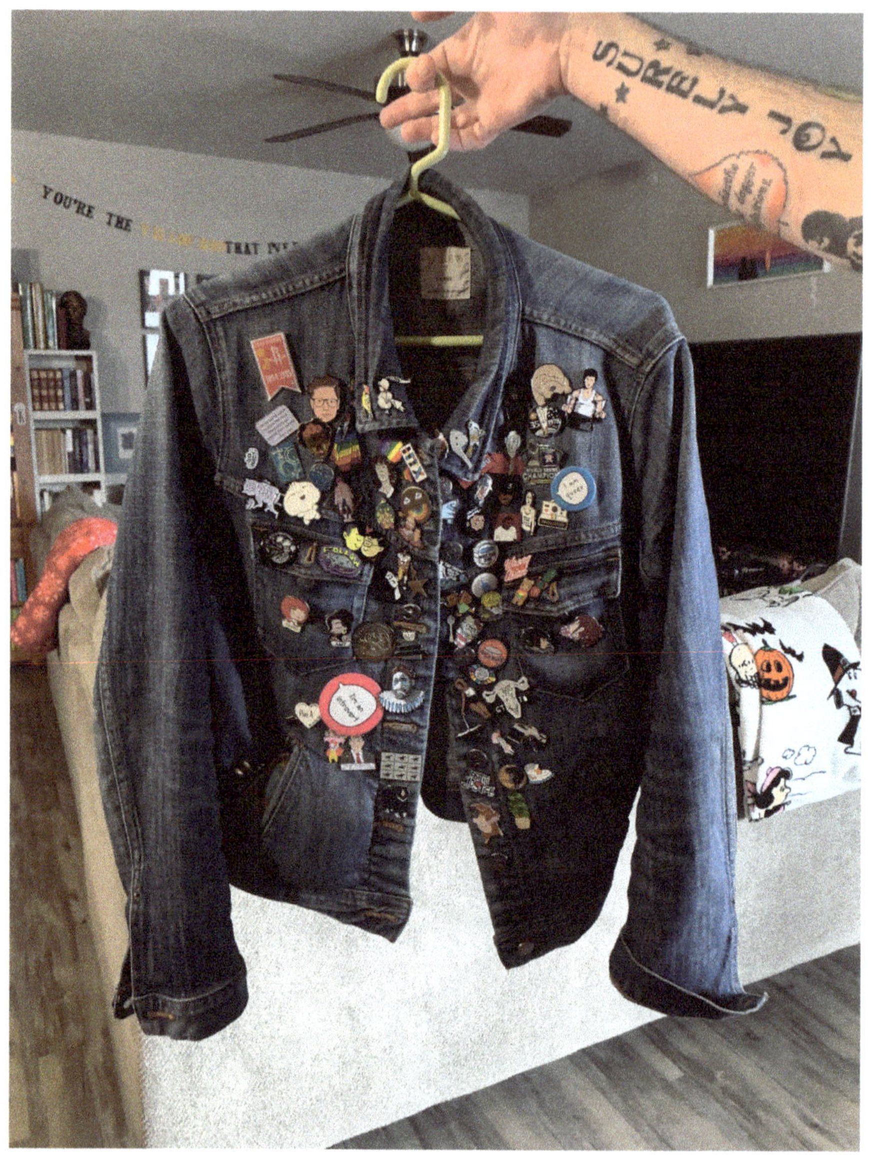

ADDIE TSAI is a queer, nonbinary artist who teaches at Houston Community College. Her queer Asian young adult novel, *Dear Twin*, is forthcoming from Metonymy Press in November 2019. She is the Nonfiction Editor at *The Grief Diaries*, Assistant Fiction Editor at *Anomaly*, Senior Associate Editor in Poetry at *The Flexible Persona*, and Senior Editor of Interviews and Culture at *Raising Mothers*.

IN PRAISE OF THE BEDAZZLED DENIM JACKET

1. The staple of all staples: the denim jacket bedazzled with buttons, patches, or in my case, the accessory that trumps all others, the lapel pin.

2. I was drawn to the denim jacket on its own on one cold November afternoon.

3. I don't have the story other queers have of their style evolution. I didn't have a father that let me run around the front lawn in my underwear and my favorite yellow rain boots. There was one morning I did, indeed, want to wear those same boots on a hot spring day. My father was a single parent, an immigrant, who must have felt it an impracticality, wearing an article of clothing purely for the look and feel of it. I hid under the bed, but eventually, I would be forced to come out and wear, again, whatever it was he had deemed appropriate.

4. My twin and I were made to dress in unison. When my father wanted to dress us as tomboys, we dressed as tomboys. When my father wanted us to wear frilly dresses in front of company, we did.

5. There are no photos I can point to, to say, there she is, desperate to come out.

6. I knew my skin tingled when I saw Whitney prance through a paint-splattered house on MTV. I knew I wanted to be seen by Janet in her *Rhythm Nation* uniform.

7. But if you were to study me, I looked like a regular old straight biracial Asian girl.

8. Before I came out: Long, dark hair. A-line skirts. Red lipstick. Mary Jane pumps. After I came out: Neon eyeliner. Bow ties. Neck ties. Oxfords. Fewer skirts. And a denim jacket gradually inking its flesh with lapel pins.

9. Number 13 on *Autostraddle's* "31 Iconic *L Word* Outfits, Ranked by Incandescence." *Buttons, Baby.* There's Shane, her usual shade of casual forlorn, a jean jacket studded with buttons. Even I, in my DIY tattooed jacket, had queered myself without realizing it.

10. This jacket is my signature brand, my identifying article, my second skin.

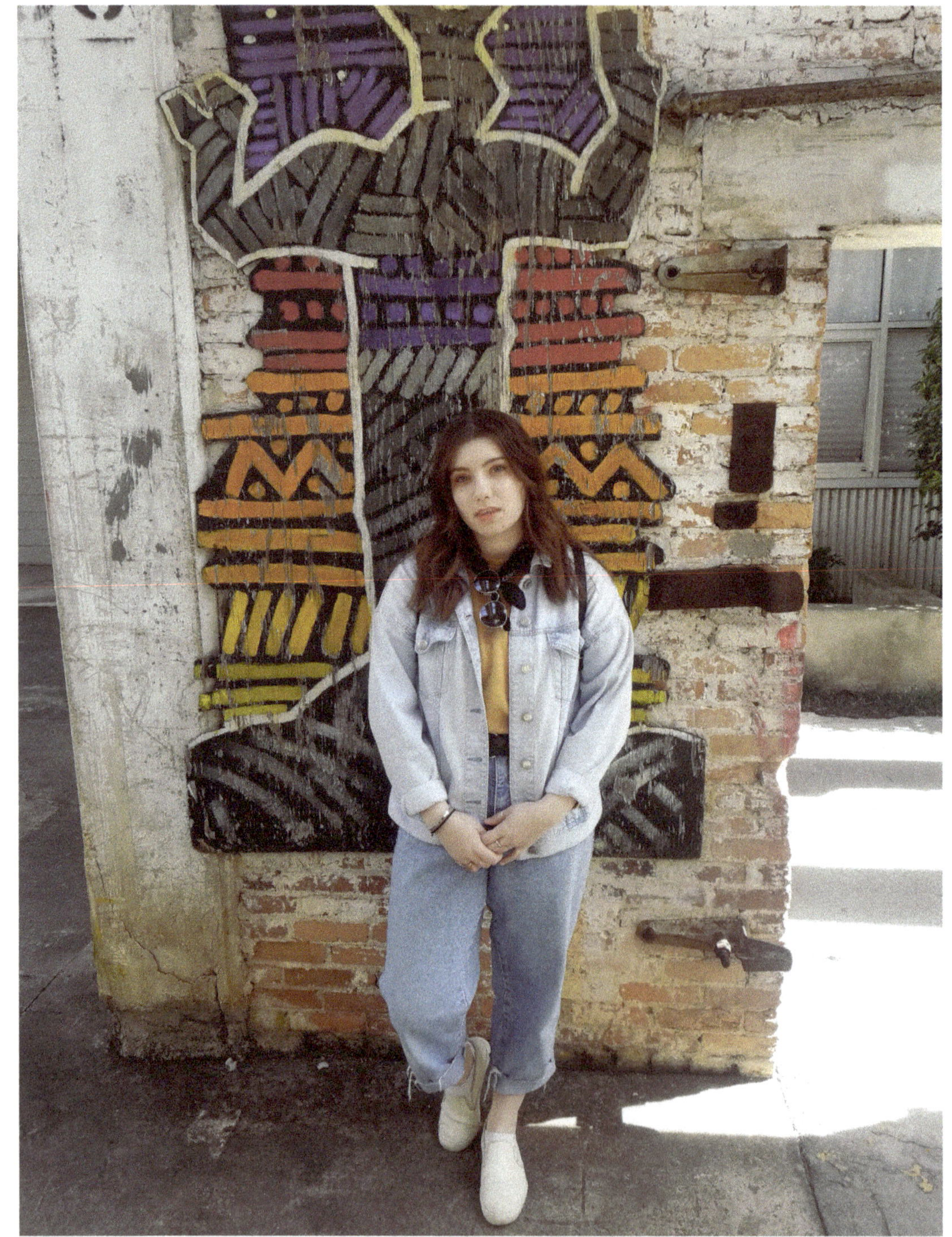

Jackets are my staple, my security blanket covering almost every favorite outfit that I style for myself. I put one on and slip into a dose of confidence. As a femme, I struggle with the in-between of feeling masculine and feminine the way I desire to. Jackets, to me, are essentially neutral and really can't be classified. I can put them with a dress and instantly make things comfier and more casual, and still have the sense of femininity. A good jacket find involves finding something that catches my eye and gets added to my mental wish list, at a thrift store or on clearance. I shop fairly green and those I like are pretty few and far between. That being said, I have been in a relationship with jackets for many years. They full on have their own closet in my house. I value them in my style more than any other item! And I am a woman of many clothes. Summers are hard for me as you can imagine. Torey in the summer feels strange, style-wise, a lot of the time, constantly wishing and waiting for that day the air drops a little cooler and I can take advantage to throw on one of my jackets, like this very loved denim!

TOREY TOMSOVIC is 26. Queer. Femme. Cis woman. Midwestern.

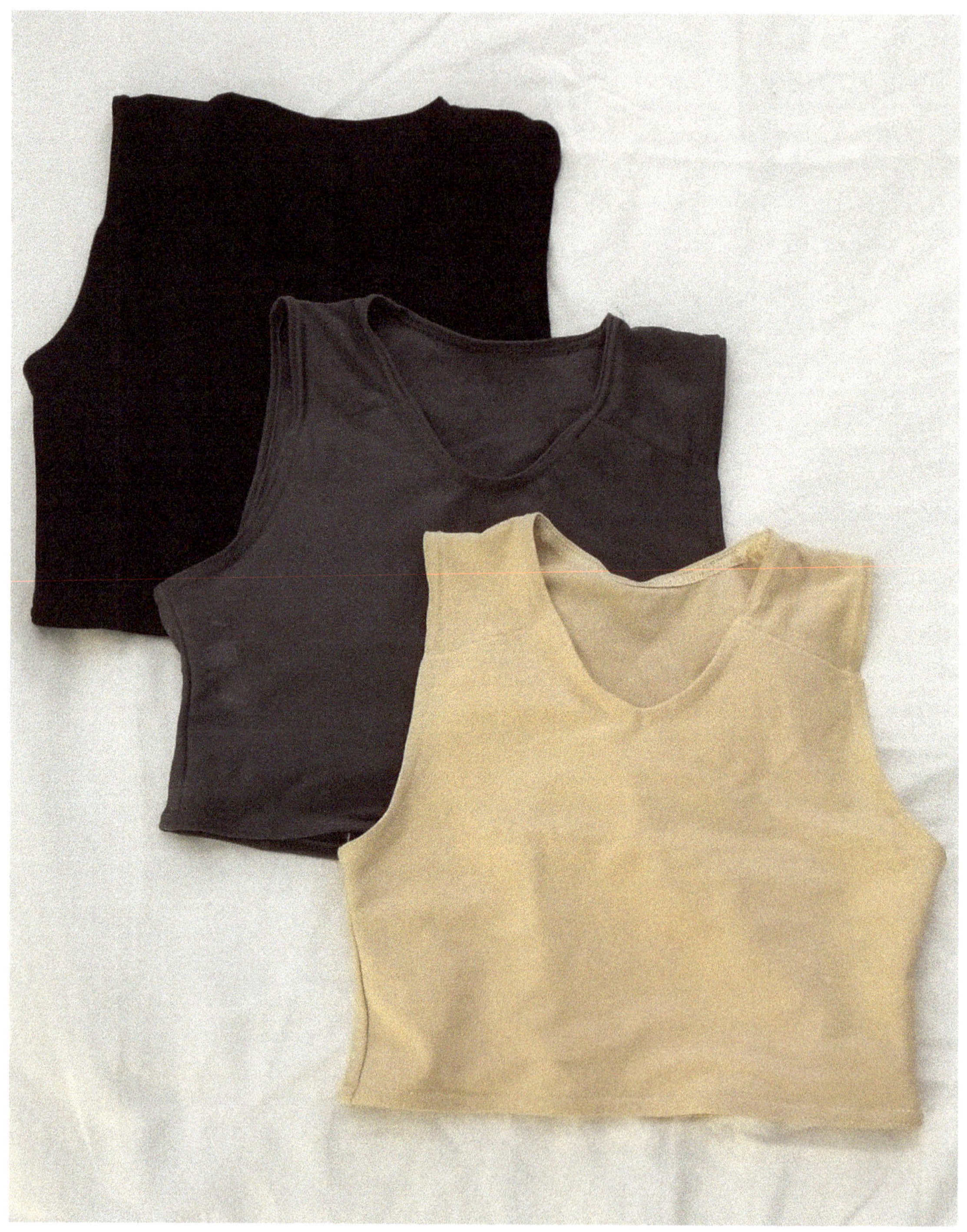

I was a freshman in college when I put on a chest binder for the first time. I'd signed up for a drag show, and if I was going to get on stage and make a fool of myself to an old Marilyn Manson song, I was at least going to look good in menswear while I did. I squirmed into the black spandex and canvas half-tank I'd bought online and was surprised at the feeling of snug pressure, like a weighted blanket for my upper half. I buttoned my shirt on over the binder, sized myself up in the mirror, and felt something click.

Womanhood always seemed a world away to me, hyper-femininity an alien custom, all for reasons I could never put into words. I tried to carve myself a tolerable, subversive niche of spikes, rips, and eyeliner, rebelling against a pink, soft, feminine ideal. When I got ready in the mornings, I floated above my body, dressing it up like a doll. The thing in front of the mirror wasn't me; its body wasn't mine.

I'd been living outside myself for years, until my first binder pressed down, flattened me out, and snapped me back into place. The night of the drag show was particularly ironic—after an endless performance in an ill-fitting role, I strutted, lip-synced, and danced my heart out onstage, and I felt more real than ever before.

After the show came and went, I still had the binder, but hadn't worn it for a bit. I'd had an excuse for it before; now, if I put it back on, it would only be because I wanted to. But what is college for, if not doing what you want?

Four years later, I own three binders that I wear regularly. I don't limit myself to menswear—my closet holds skirts, combat boots, neckties, and glittery lip gloss, the nest of a gender magpie hoarding pretty scraps. My binders are special, though. Without them I may never have strayed off womanhood's beaten path. I still laugh at their name sometimes. My chest is bound. I'm free.

ROWAN THOMPSON is a graduate of the University of Georgia and a fiction writer, artist, and collector of button pins.

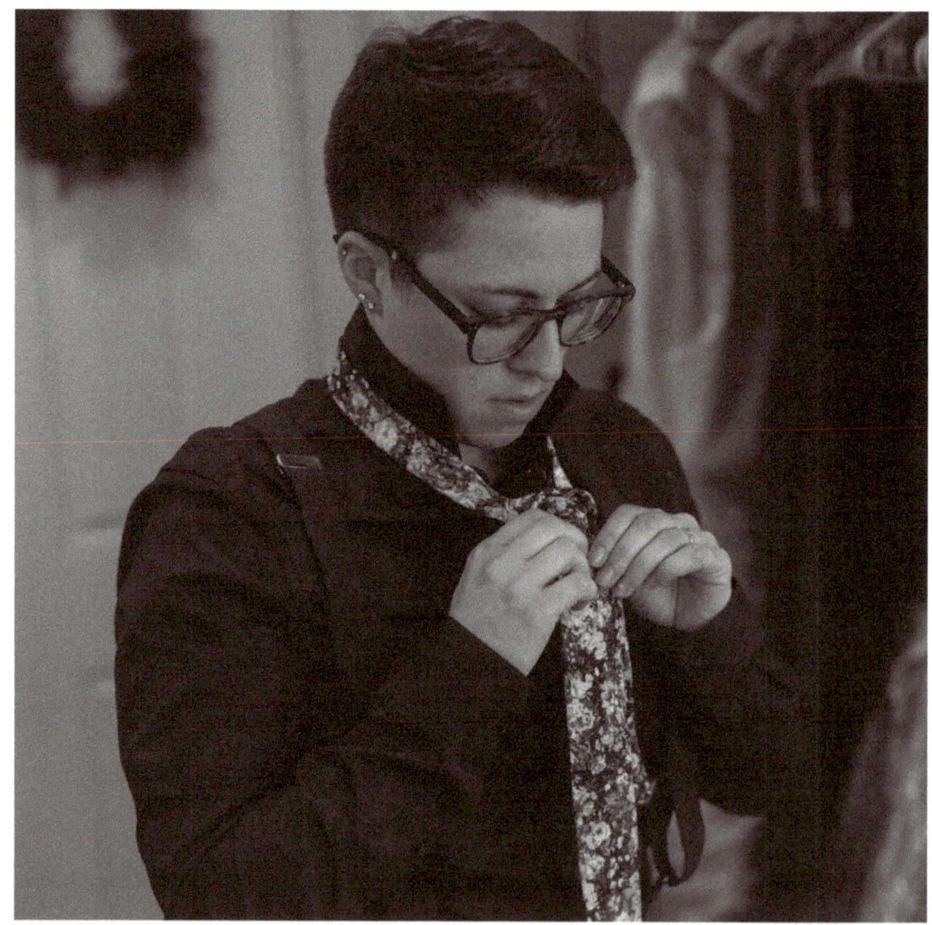

JULES TAYLOR is a high school English teacher and MFA student at Reinhardt University. She lives in Decatur, Georgia, with her dog, Archer.

THE CLOTHES I WEAR

You resent the way I look, saying,
　　　You are making a statement,
　　　nose crinkled in distaste.

The knotting of
this floral tie
around my neck,
the deep-ocean blue suspenders
that waterfall and curve
over my feminine chest
are not about
　　　you.
It's not about how "gay" I can look
so I can watch discomfort
spread across your face.

I wear this suit and tie to officiate a wedding,
　　　to celebrate a love full of mutual weirdness.

The best man helped me tighten the knot before the ceremony,
　　　thumped my shoulders and said,
　　　　　You look dapper as fuck.

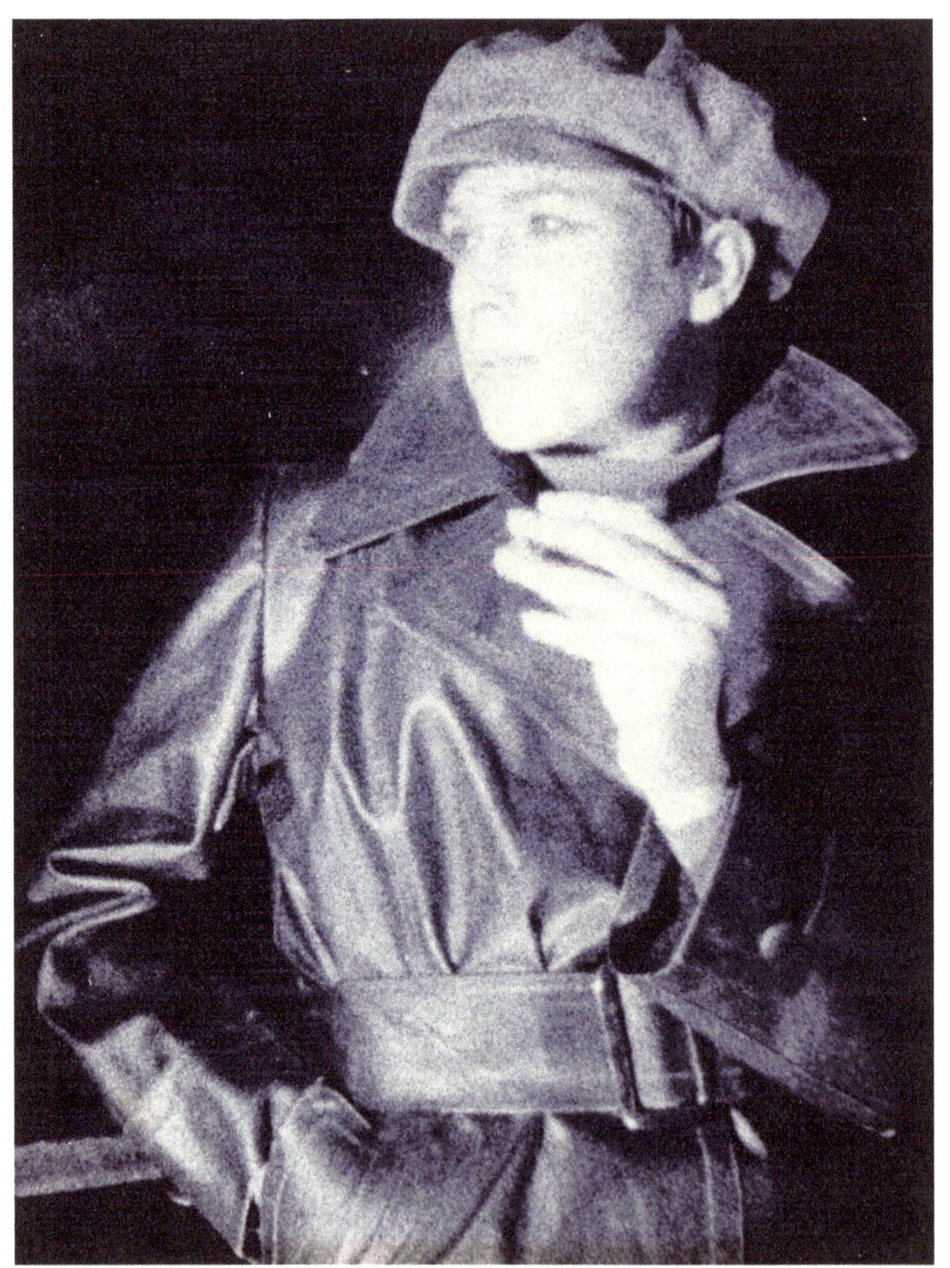

It was the end of my first year in Paris. While Stéphane was doing *théâtre d'action*, political street theater, I took ballet classes at Place Clichy, a building with several dance studios, creaking stairs, huge, unwashed windows, and tiny, sweat-soaked dressing rooms. Day after day I walked through the political unrest of the student revolts, literally walked through half of Paris, as there were no metros or buses running. After a few weeks, the streets up to Clichy were lined with mountains of garbage so high you could no longer see the third-floor windows of the houses. Everyone supported the general strike and most cars took up pedestrians wherever they could be seen walking.

I used to wear a long, belted military-style coat and a self-made street-boy's cap. Drivers would lean out of their car windows and shout, "*Hé, gavroche,* want a ride?" Being called "street urchin" in French was a *tendresse,* a compliment, and I usually followed the invitations, even though there wasn't a single time that I didn't have to go into laborious battles to fight off the men's seduction. It forced me to speak with a certain speed and panache. I took it as a sport, a contrast to my mostly nonverbal days of ballet training, getting special lessons in French flirting.

RENATE STENDHAL was a lesbian-feminist of the first hour in Paris, France. She is a German-born writer, writing coach, and interpersonal counselor in the San Francisco Bay Area. Her recent memoir, *Kiss Me Again, Paris,* was a Lambda literary finalist and won two awards. She has published six books in the US, among them, the photo biography *Gertrude Stein: in Words and Pictures.* With her spouse, Kim Chernin, she wrote *Lesbian Marriage: A Love & Sex Survival Kit,* and she published the couples guide *True Secrets of Lesbian Desire: How to Keep Sex Alive in Long-Term Relationships.*

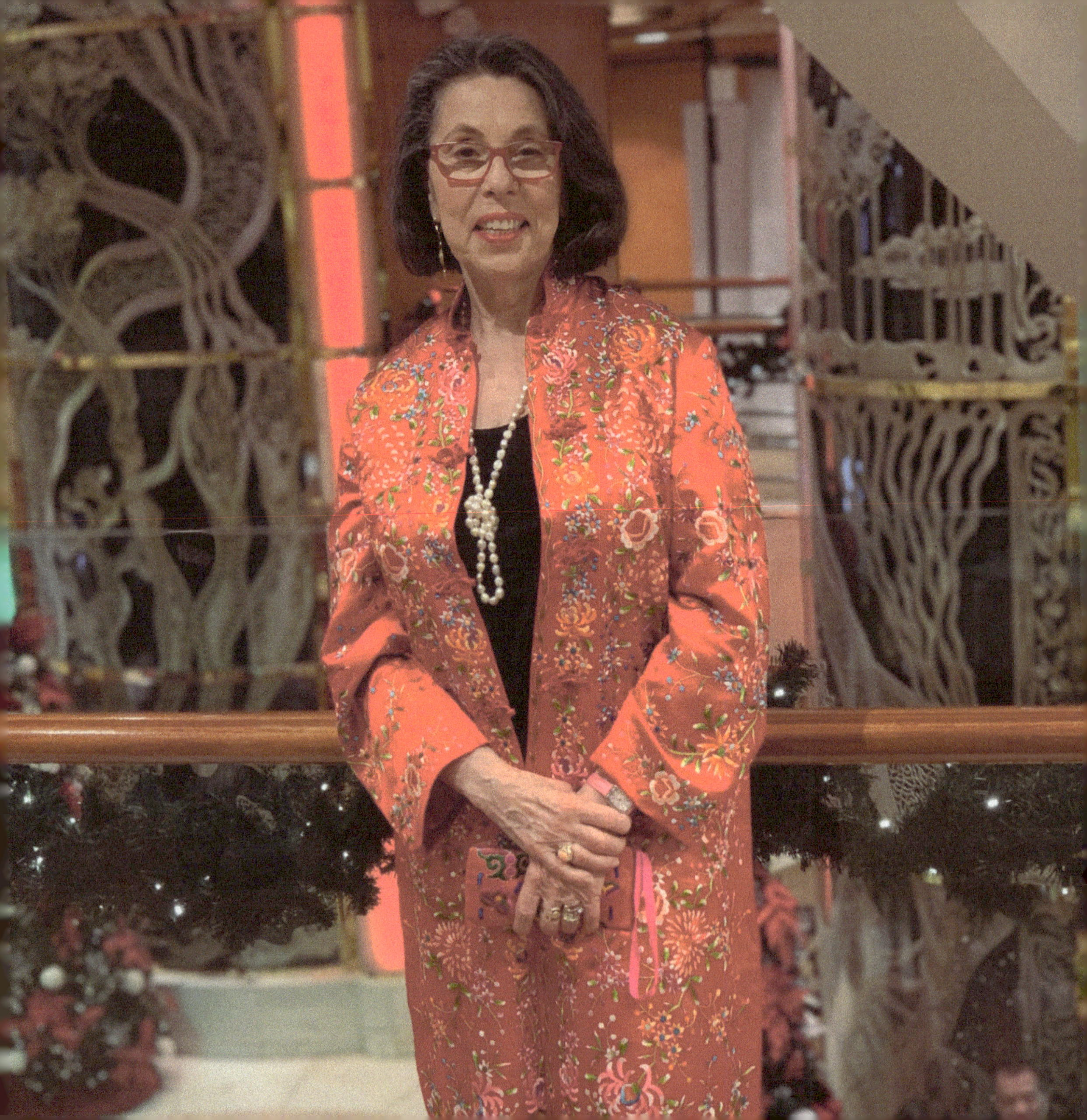

My mother loved to travel. In 1973, soon after Nixon opened the door to China, my parents went there. One of the things they brought back was this hand-embroidered silk coat. I have been wearing it on special occasions for more than 40 years. The coat may be in better shape than I am. In this photograph, I am wearing it on Christmas Eve, 2018, aboard a ship in the Gulf of Thailand.

By happenstance, there were at least forty-five LGBTQ+ people on this cruise ship. We found each other within a couple of days of leaving Singapore and met each evening for drinks and laughs. On Christmas Eve, we all sat together in the dining room.

I bought the pearls I'm wearing at the Ben Thanh Market in Saigon (that's what locals still seem to call it, not Ho Chi Minh City). Two of the couples and I had signed up for a one-day cooking course with a chef at the Rex Hotel. We were at the market selecting ingredients when I spotted the pearl dealers. I have a "thing" for pearls. I have nineteen pearl necklaces of various lengths, sizes, and quality. My fashion inspiration in this regard is Queen Elizabeth I. Now *those* are pearls.

ANNA SEQUOIA is the author of ten nonfiction books, including the animal rights classic *67 Ways to Save the Animals* (Harper Perennial), and the best-selling humor book, *The Official J.A.P. Handbook* (N.A.L.). Anna has appeared on more than one hundred radio and television programs. A recent article about her cooking/entertaining dubbed her "the Jewish Martha Stewart." She is married to Una Fahy.

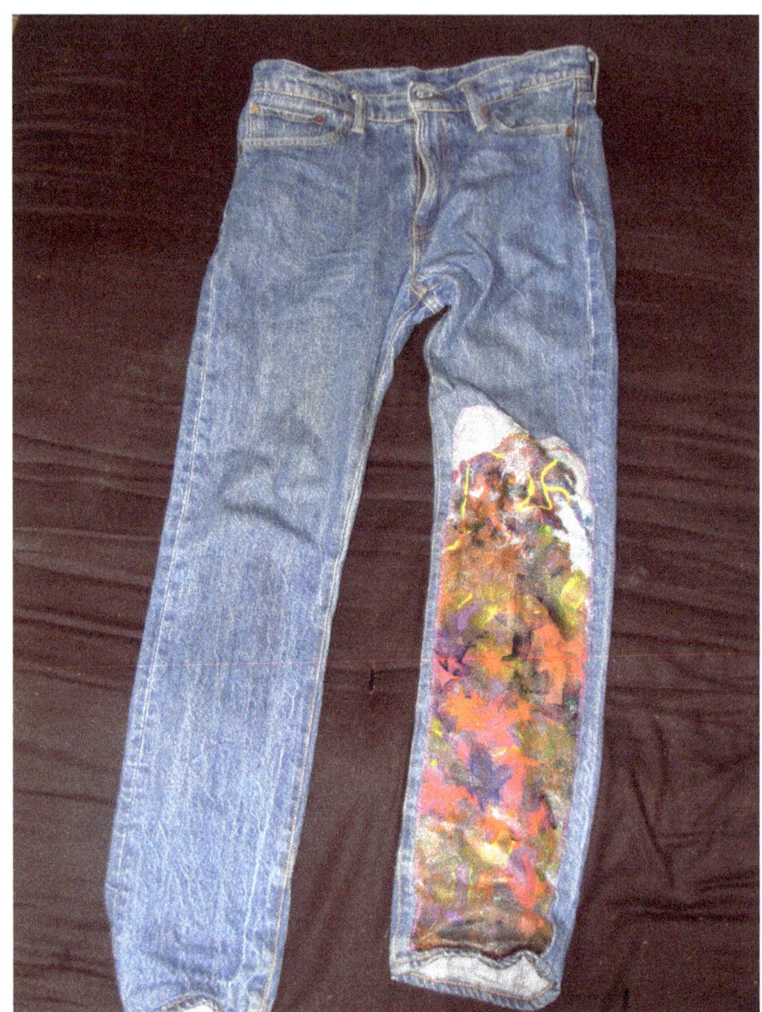

EVA M. SCHLESINGER is a recipient of the Literal Latte Food Verse Award and a two-time Moth StorySlam winner. She is the author of *Remembering the Walker & Wheelchair: poems of grief and healing* (Finishing Line Press, 2008) and three dancing girl press titles, for which she designed the covers: *View From My Banilla Vanilla Villa* (2010), *Ode 2 Codes & Codfish* (2013), and *Ninnies Who Whinny* (2017). Her work has appeared in a variety of publications, including the *San Francisco Chronicle*, *Hashtag Queer*, *Changing Harm to Harmony: Bullies & Bystanders Project*, and *Women in Clothes*.

TRANSFORMING ANGER TO BEAUTY

I had never painted my clothes before. I thought it'd be fun to try. I also thought it'd be a good way to channel the anger I felt about making a mistake at work the day before. I had been raised to be a perfectionist. I also had been raised to express only happy feelings, not sad; never mad.

I decided to depict a dog on the lower leg of my jeans. I had grown up with a white-haired, shaggy, furry dog friend who comforted me throughout my childhood. But what I painted looked nothing like a dog.

I added more colors. My dog was a messy clump of paint. I mashed down the colors with my fingers. I mooshed the colors. I smooshed them. I folded the edges of my pant leg inward and pounded the material with my fists.

When I unfolded the sides, swirls of color burst out, soothing me. Thanks to the anger about my mistake, I had created beauty.

That was twenty-eight years ago. I have since transferred the design twice to new pairs of jeans. I've also strived to embrace my feelings and mistakes.

I wear these jeans when I want to be outspoken and visible. Of all my painted clothing, these win the most compliments.

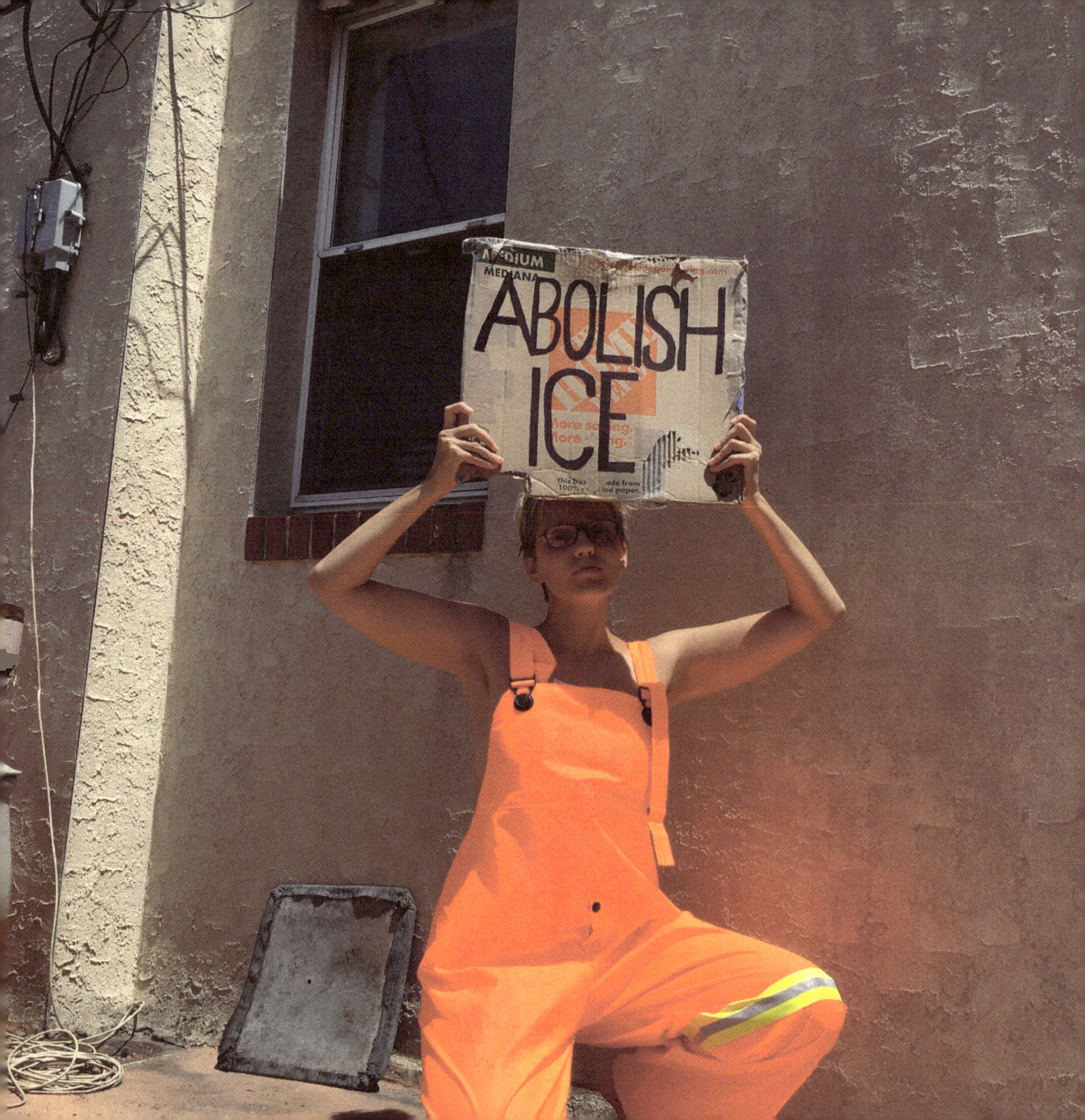

MEDIUM
MEDIANA
ABOLISH
ICE
More saving.
More doing.
This box made from
100% recycled paper.

DYKE MARCH

Philly's dyke march has been going since 1998. Every year, it's billed as a protest NOT a parade, keeping pride's roots in queer riot. We march through Center City Philadelphia without a permit. Tourists and wealthy residents tend to gawk. We chant, we hold signs, we bare skin. We include ALL self-identified dykes.

Like lots of queers, for years I used clothes to hide. Working as a domestic employee with a creep for an employer, I tucked myself into baggy wear. I hid out. It didn't stop the guy from groping me.

Years later I tried on my first latex at a great sex store on South Street. The person who was helping me was relieved to notice my super short nails because it meant the latex was less likely to tear. Short nails are imperative— nothing to do with style.

In the latex I felt held and taut. It was slippery and tight. I felt like a seal in heat. Like I'd tucked. Like a gender deviant. The top I liked was $209— way too much for me to afford.

A week later my friend gave me used latex coveralls they didn't need anymore. These were nothing like the latex in the sex shop. They were fluorescent orange and didn't cinch. They were clothes for working and for staying highly visible. The fluorescence screamed WATCH OUT: EMERGENCY.

Capitalism creates constant crises but the crises themselves are real. That year, the dyke march occupied the streets with calls to abolish ICE, to close U.S. detention centers, to end family separation, and to abolish borders.

The gifted latex made me feel less like a seal in heat and more like an urgent, flashing EMERGENCY sign. Like a gender abolitionist. Like a busy street overtaken by dykes in protest.

EMMA BROWN SANDERS is a queer, nonbinary poet living in Philadelphia. Their work can be found in *Bedfellows, Bone Bouquet, Boneless Skinless, Fungiculture, Prolit, Reflections on the Burden of Men, Tripwire,* and *the tiny,* among others. They have been nominated for Pushcart and Bettering American Poetry prizes.

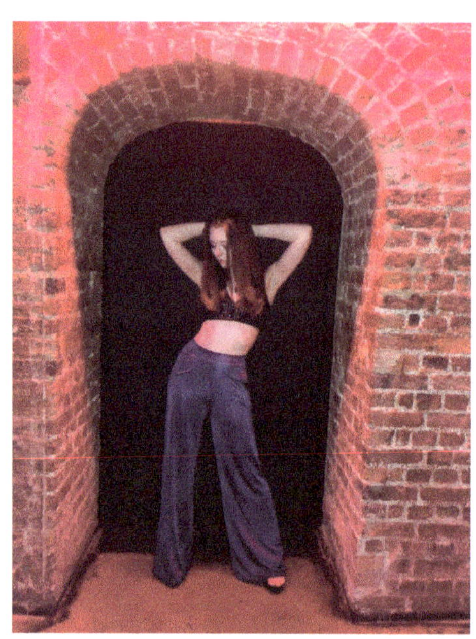

LUCY HANNAH RYAN is a poet, diarist, and short story writer from London. Her work often concerns femininity, sexuality, and complex relationships with the body inspired by her experience with chronic illnesses and pain. She has been published in *Poetry Quarterly*, *Vitality Magazine*, and *Half Mystic*, among others, and was a winner in the London *City of Stories* competition 2018.

I PUT ON SOME INDIGO TROUSERS AND THINK I'M GIRL POSEIDON

there's sweet comfort in the vitality of water, the way it swallows the body and yet parts around it. marble and satin can both contain a softened flow—I dressed myself for Ophelia tonight.

here is the drowning fantasy against the potential of cresting waves—held above or moving through it, and baby I am godless god & I move like the sea. I love to slip into the flow, to clasp it around the waist—to wear the killing thing and stand taller than the sky. rising against the weary stone of the body, the artifice of strength beneath the perceived softness of a riverbed. maybe the body aches, maybe the armour buoys it.

roll with me, then, the hips rippling into sweet waves, the movement mermaid or starving siren. I am satin, smooth, fluid; on the rise and bracing for vibrant crash.

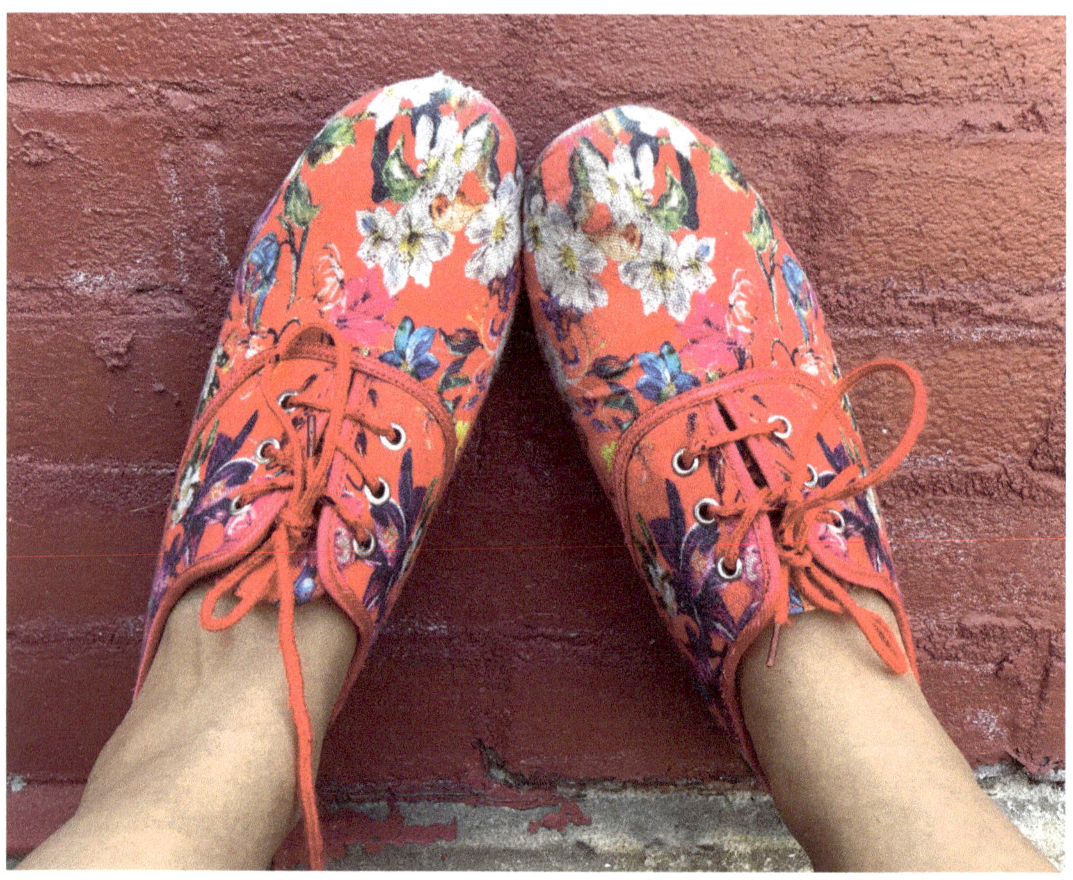

LAUREN RUSSELL is the author of *What's Hanging on the Hush* (Ahsahta Press, 2017), and *Descent* (Tarpaulin Sky Press, 2020), co-winner of the 2019 Tarpaulin Sky Book Awards. She has received fellowships from the NEA, Cave Canem, and the Wisconsin Institute for Creative Writing, and her work has appeared in *The New York Times Magazine*, *Bettering American Poetry 2015*, and the Academy of American Poets *Poem-a-Day*, among others. She is a research assistant professor in English and is assistant director of the Center for African American Poetry and Poetics at the University of Pittsburgh. The quotation in this text is from Russell's introduction for Saretta Morgan at a reading held at Alphabet City in Pittsburgh on February 15, 2019.

TO REDLY TREAD

My red flower-power shoes
are armor from stampeding
doubts, they're zippy
cooler-than-thou lace-up
Mardi Gras, larks' botanical
canvas resthomes, footnests
fleeced from Marie Antoinette's
footrests, Oscar Wilde's cast-
off carnation lapels. My footsore
feet soar bootie up for super-
glued soles, snug as rosebeds smug
as well-heeled thorns.

I once described my relationship to autumn: "Often in the fall . . . I feel hyper-vulnerable, porous, like a sieve, so that everybody else's feelings seem to penetrate my borders and my own seep out in reckless, unwieldly excretions that impede movement, puddling at my feet." In order to move, I need superpower shoes. I ordered these from the Victorian Trading Company in the fall of 2017, the fall I learned that my cat, Neruda, was dying. Neruda was my constant companion, familiar, and friend across twelve apartments in three states. I adopted him after a series of psychiatric hospitalizations, as a commitment to life.

In grief my feet schlepp through autumn muck adorned in red.

I have struggled with depression on and off for most of my life. I have likened it to living under a lead blanket or in an infinite black tunnel with no sign of light. My depression feels devoid of color—or maybe it is more like all the colors splattering, congealing into muck. I wear red as an act of resistance against despair. I wear reds in all shades and weights, the whole family of red—orange, purple, hot pink, violet. I drape them all over my body so that if I pass a mirror or glance down at my feet, my life under the lead blanket in the black tunnel can still contain a shimmer of delight. Like poetry and cats, red is a life force, so I wear it with humility. When someone tells me I look good in red, I say *Maybe red looks good on me.*

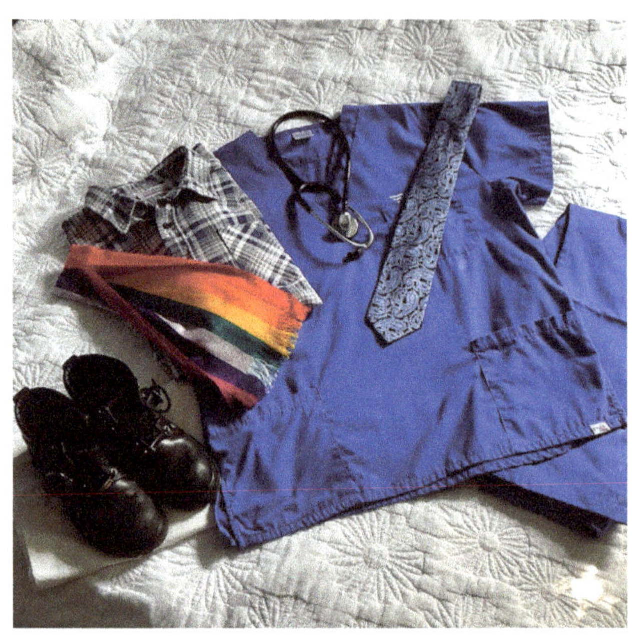

RANDI ROMO is a 63-year-old, Mexican/American, Southern Dyke, born in Dallas and currently residing in Little Rock, Arkansas. With a 6th grade education, she is a self-taught writer—queerness disrupting her access to a formal education. Romo's work has been featured in various publications. Her short stories were presented on the *Tales from the South* radio show and podcast. Her first book, *Othered* (Sibling Rivalry, 2018), was selected by the American Library Association as a top-five book in poetry/fiction for 2018 in its annual Over the Rainbow List of Recommended LGBTQ Reading.

SCRUB LIFE

Your hand cups my elbow, as I lean in
steely fangs at the ready, piercing you
for the third time this week, like clockwork
Monday, Wednesday, and Friday, you sit
as I pull your blood through this miracle
of plastic tubing, an extracorporeal circuit
an extra chance to remain of this world

The intimacy of this ritual, of saving your life
would it be enough for you to save mine,
I find myself wondering, my queerness evident
short hair, tattoos, all butchona, but we don't
speak of it, many of you with bibles in tow
belated quest for salvation or making peace
for the inevitable, the final bow, in this end stage

If you saw me, dress shirt and tie, or wearing my
favorite flannel shirt, jeans, and my Harley boots
maybe I've got on the rainbow scarf that I love
to wear while reading my super gay, lesbionic
poetic musings that talk a lot about the pain inflicted
would you quote your scripture, refuse my care
though I've been awash in your blood so many times

Would you care as much for my life, as I do yours . . .
    If you truly saw the all of me

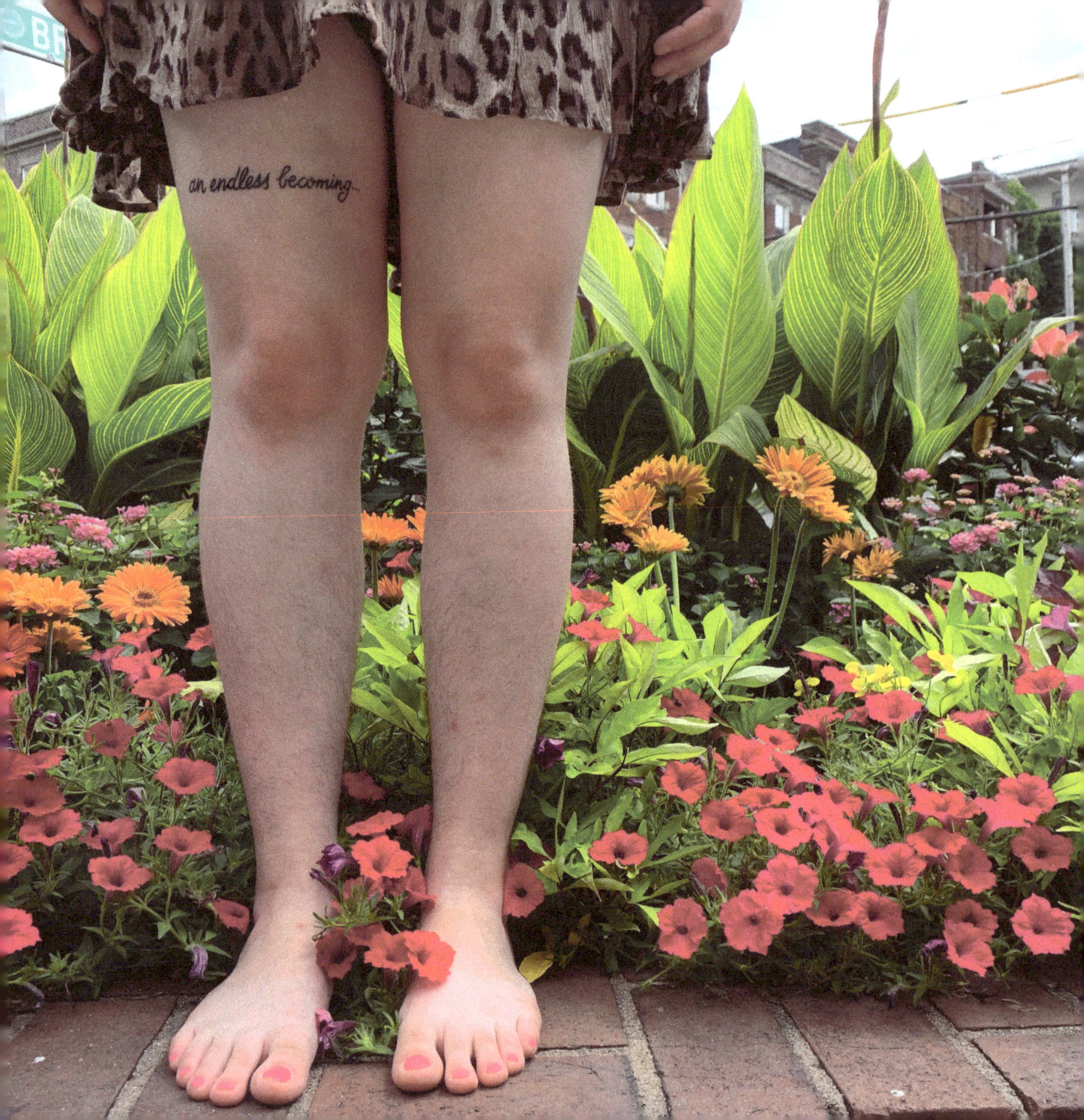
an endless becoming...

I started a new job at a prestigious university and an IT guy in his fifties with too-strong cologne came to set up my computer. In the midst of telling me about his four ex-wives, he said:

"I don't want to be creepy, but I find your leg hair incredibly sexy."

I blanched. My hairy legs were crisscrossed on my desk chair, the fabric of my leopard dress pooled in my lap. Five years of au naturel growth had been for my own comfort, not his gaze. I couldn't very well say *Fuck you* in this professional environment. I untangled my legs, smoothed down my dress, and told him the truth in the hopes it would shut him up:

"My hairy legs allow other women to know I'm queer despite the fact I wear dresses and lipstick."

Thankfully, he took my response as a rebuff and stayed silent.

My femme identity, paired with the fact I often date cis-men, means my queerness is nearly invisible—except for the days I can wear an outfit that shows off my leg hair.

When I was growing up, my mom's friends who identified as lesbians were far more likely to have unshaved armpits and legs than her straight friends. The queer female staff at my childhood summer camp (where I shared my first kisses with other girls) also tended to be much hairier than their straight counterparts. I came to understand body hair as both a rejection of heterosexual patriarchal beauty ideals *and* a visual signifier of female queerness.

I wish I could have told the IT guy how violated I felt by his sexualization of my leg hair. I wish I could have communicated how my hairy legs display a crucial part of my identity. I wish he could understand how amazing the wind feels when it blows through my leg hair, as if there are a thousand tiny *thank yous* sending warm tingles across my skin. But instead of wasting my energy, I reported him to HR so another woman with hairy legs doesn't have to deal with his bullshit.

RAINA K. PUELS is a queer, poly human living in Boston with her cat, Layla Stoner Sparkle Demon. You can read her writing in *GAY Mag*, *The Rumpus*, *PANK*, and many other publications listed on her website, rainakpuels.com. Follow her on Instagram to hear about her Astrological Emergencies.

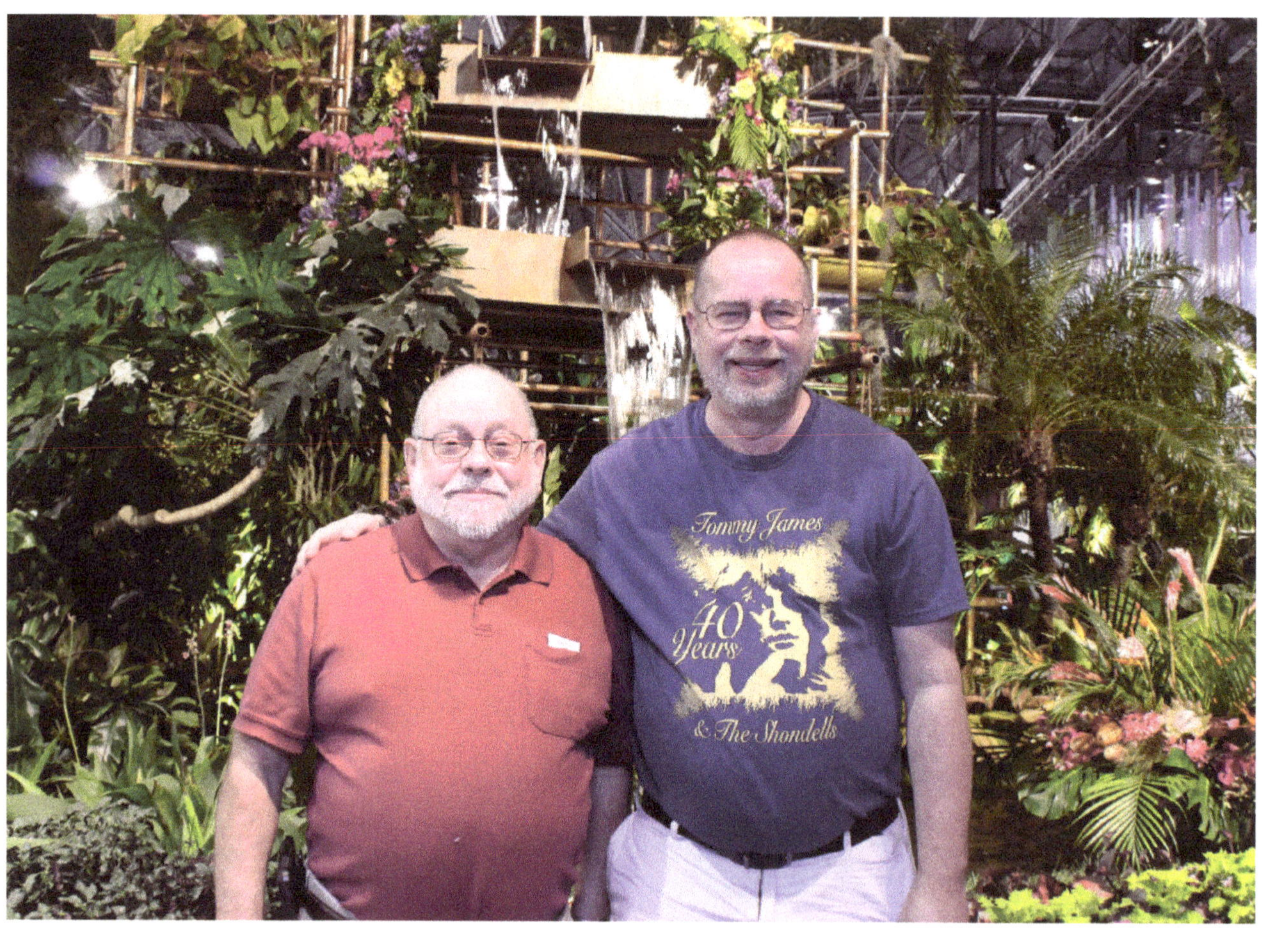

KENNETH POBO has a new book of prose poems called *The Antlantis Hit Parade* (Clare Song-birds Publishing House, 2019). Also published in 2019 is *Dindi Expecting Snow* (Duck Lake Books).

40 YEARS

At the Philadelphia Flower Show,
orchids are like Mrs. Drysdale, proud,
demanding attention. In my
Tommy James & The Shondells 40 Years

t-shirt, I'm back in 1966, 11 years old,
"Hanky Panky" on my transistor radio.
I didn't understand people doing
the hanky panky, it sounded fun,
but I rode my bike up to Ben Franklin's
for snow cones. Sex,
a rumor the other kids spread.
Gay sex, don't talk about it,
don't think about it, turn it
into a joke, an insult—there's only
one way to do the hanky panky.

Decades crash against the rail
of my life. Do Stan and I
do it wrong?

The lyrics say, "Hey pretty baby
can I take you home?" We head
for the train, then home—cats
clatter down wooden stairs and a bashful
Christmas cactus slowly opens
a coral bud.

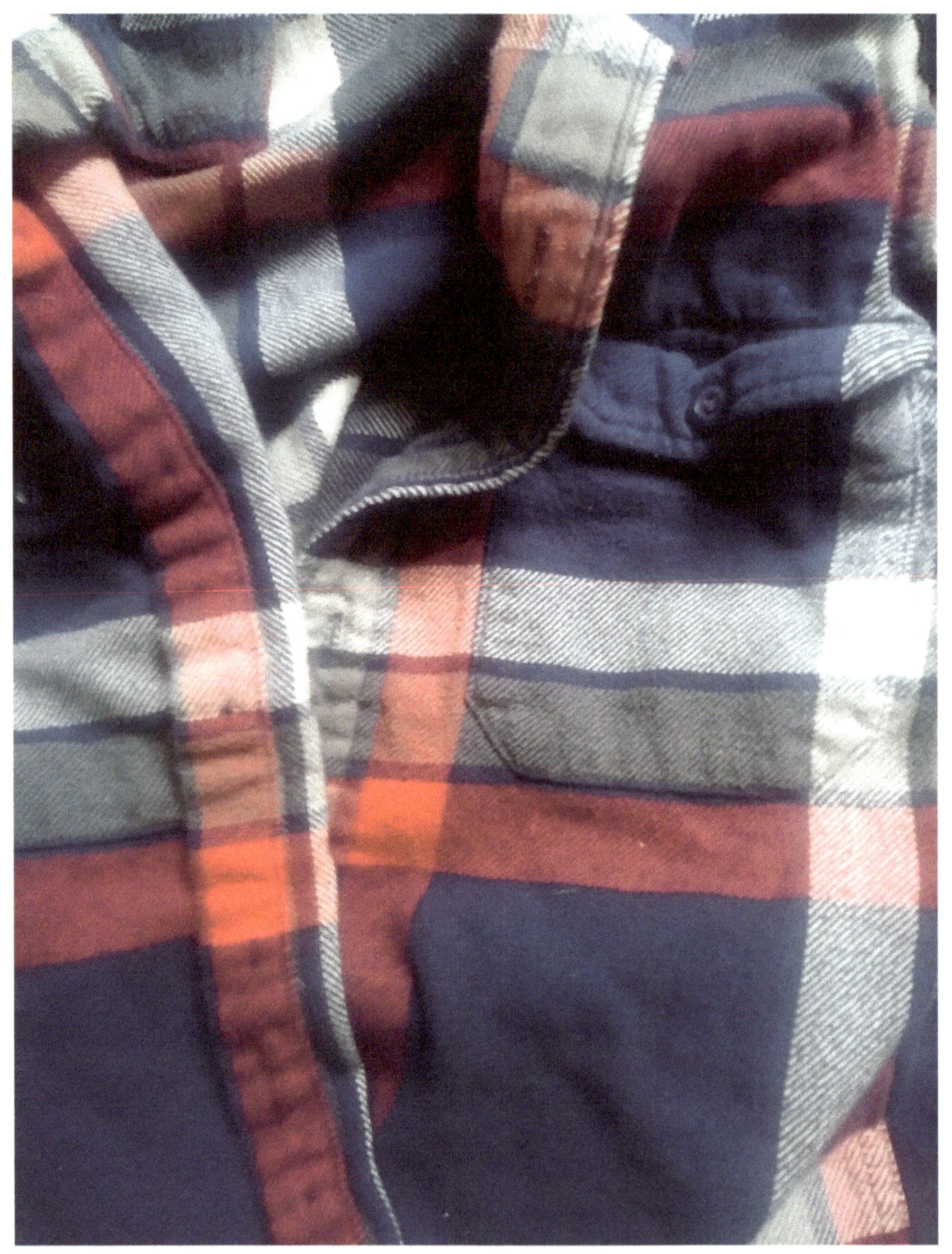

NINA PICK is an oral historian, book editor, and teacher who lives in New York.

THE FLANNEL SHIRT

When I was in my early twenties and living in San Francisco, I had trouble identifying myself within the queer community. With my wide hips and curly hair, I couldn't help but look femme no matter what I wore. But I never felt comfortable in feminine clothing, even in early childhood (one of my earliest memories is fighting with my mother as she tried to dress me for school), and I preferred an androgynous look, which was confusing because most of the women I was attracted to—that is to say, obsessed with—seemed to prefer femme women. I remember thinking there was a marked division between the categories of femme, butch, and androgynous, and I didn't belong in any of these boxes. I felt like some kind of weird insect, unable to signify that it was available to mate.

Then I found flannel, and all my dilemmas were answered. In a flannel shirt I could look queer, pass for straight, and radiate femme, butch, and androgynous, all at the same time. When I went to visit my parents back East, I felt right at home hanging out at the bar with the local farmers, for whom flannel was practically a uniform. It reminded me of bonfires and the smell of early spring. Simultaneously tough and soft, it curled around my body like a warm hug.

When I got sober at twenty-five, I wore flannel through the six months of the immobilizing anxiety and depression that accompanied early recovery. I wore it all day in bed and across the city to therapy. Later, I wore it to the San Francisco Zen Center and to Sha'ar Zahav, a wonderful queer synagogue. I wore it back to grad school to finish my master's, to the beach in Point Reyes, and on dates with other sober people. I wore it into a new life.

Eventually I moved back to the East Coast, and a year later met my partner. Early on in our relationship, I gave him an old flannel I had been holding on to for years despite that fact that it was pink, splattered in paint, and so large it went down almost to my knees. It fit him perfectly, and he loved it. I, in turn, loved him for being a man comfortable in a pink shirt.

When we moved in together, I quickly realized that a perk of the arrangement (among other delights) is that I have access to an entire wardrobe of men's clothing. Sometimes we laugh as we leave the house because we realize we're wearing the same outfit. When I walk in the woods near our apartment, my flannel reminds me of my own queer, transitory, and multiple nature. It reminds me of how far I've come and who I've become. The poet Ellery Akers writes, in one of my favorite lines, "When I look at my life I can see a sane woman / walking through blunt grass." I am similarly grateful to be able to look at myself in the mirror and see a sober woman wearing a man's shirt.

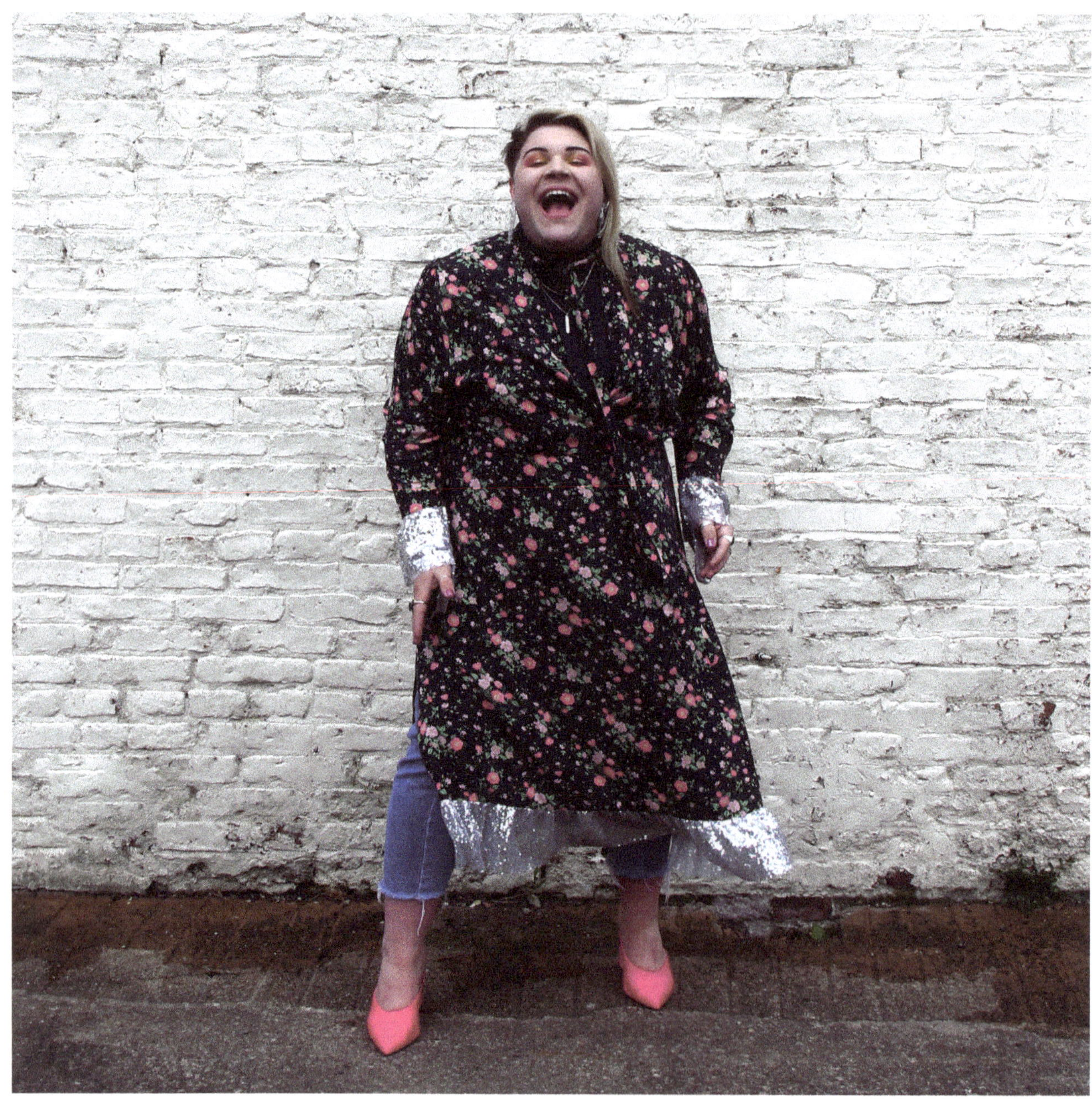

Dressing as a non-binary person is incredibly powerful, yet also an act of defiance. You are admitting to yourself that you are in full control of your gender identity, and the freedom that realisation provides makes you feel light and joyous.

By choosing to dress like this I am subverting all the binary gender assumptions and behaviours that have held most civilisations together for millennia. It must be noted that the defiance in wearing a dress does not go unnoticed or unpunished. I am subjected to a barrage of stares, personal comments, and anger from complete strangers, which by now I am aware comes with the territory.

One of my favourite garments is a dress. It says an awful lot about my gender identity, which sits very happily in the middle of the mélange of predicted gender assumptions and behaviours. A dress is very freeing for me, as typically this piece of cloth is regarded as female only; thus in donning this garment I am expressing my stance on myself and the world around me.

Day to day, I am not making a political statement or even trying to cause a reaction; I am just having fun in dressing as I feel. I don't believe there to be a greater feeling than a joyous outfit making you smile all day long, which this dress really does. Essentially, this dress is an extension of my sense of self and my personality right now.

This dress, in particular, is like a Madonna mega-mix—all the best things thrown together. All at once, it is amazing and just a little bit too much. Bringing sequins galore, a chintzy floral pattern that I find comforting, a tie neck that makes me feel so secure, and finally the all-important leg slit.

I adore the way this dress, and all dresses, make me feel. A true sense of freedom cannot be bought, but to me, a dress unlocks the ability to feel truly free in my soul, and for that, it is genuinely priceless and precious!

BEN PECHEY is a freelance writer, fashion critic, proud Leo, and LGBTQ+ activist in the United Kingdom. Growing up, they never saw or knew anybody like themself. Now they are incredibly comfortable with who they are and are visibly present in society. They are existing and thriving as a member of the LGBTQ+ community. They hope that they can be the representation for people just like them, giving all the chance to feel the acceptance that they so often struggled to feel growing up.

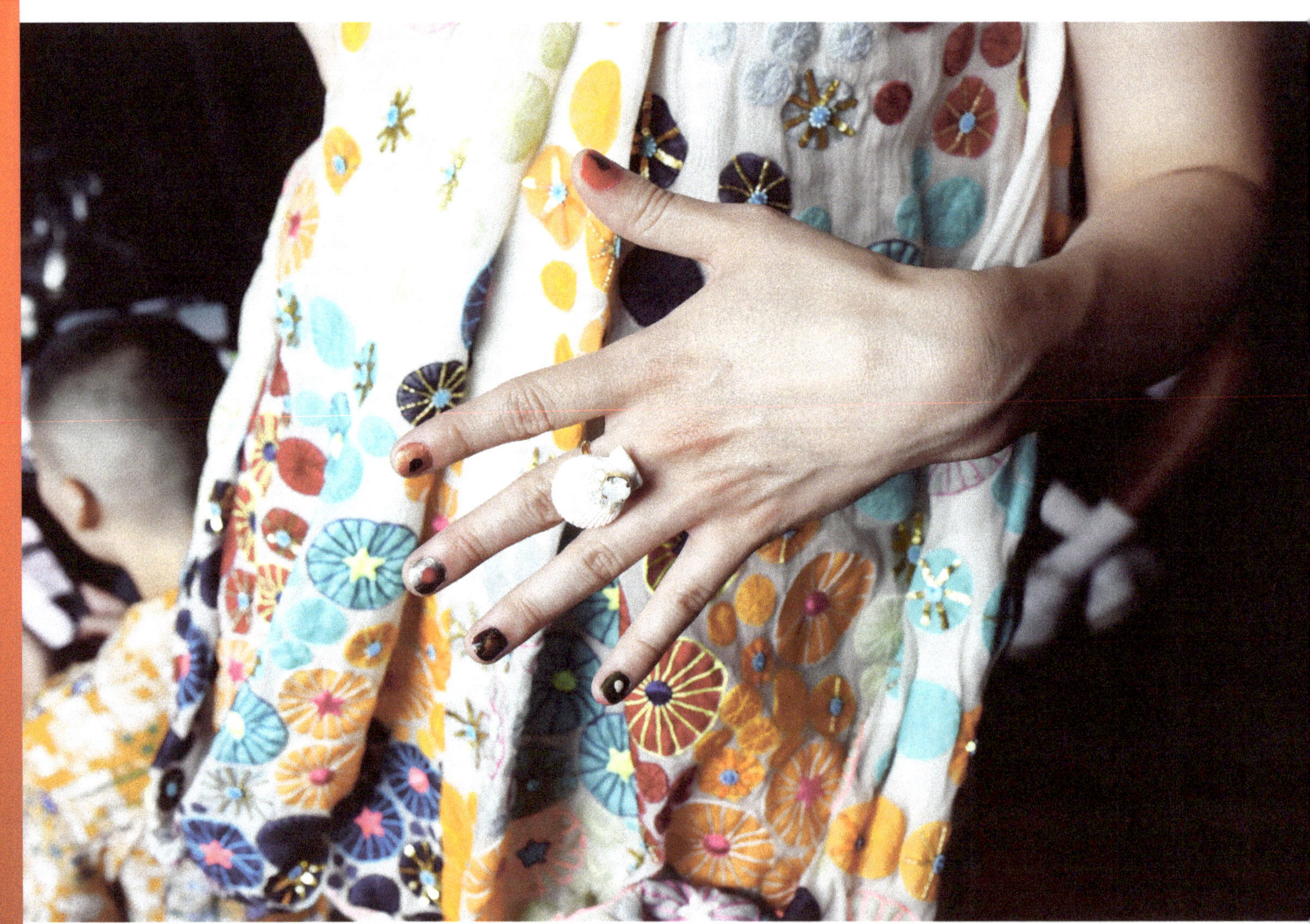

CAKED & CODED

On femme visibility . . . because it's not just about a cute look or bold style, but a coded sartorial language that's innately subversive: I love layering patterns and infusing unexpected palettes for a look that's puzzling to the male gaze while pleasing to the queer eye. Color meets print in dizzying proportions and silhouettes to irritate notions of eclectic glamor.

It's an obfuscation of normative erogenous zones that I've unconsciously guarded through my posture and gait.

I love heavy doses of high-octane statements within the climate of fast fashion because it's an affordable systemic rejection of a heteropatriarchal system. My femme identity lives within the cloth I wear on my back, the jewels that gleam on my neck, and the shimmery shadows baked into my skin.

CHRISTIANE NICKEL is a femme dyke fashion historian/copywriter who is half German/American and enjoys long workouts on the beach and countless hours of *Real Housewives*. Photo by Jacenne Lemonne.

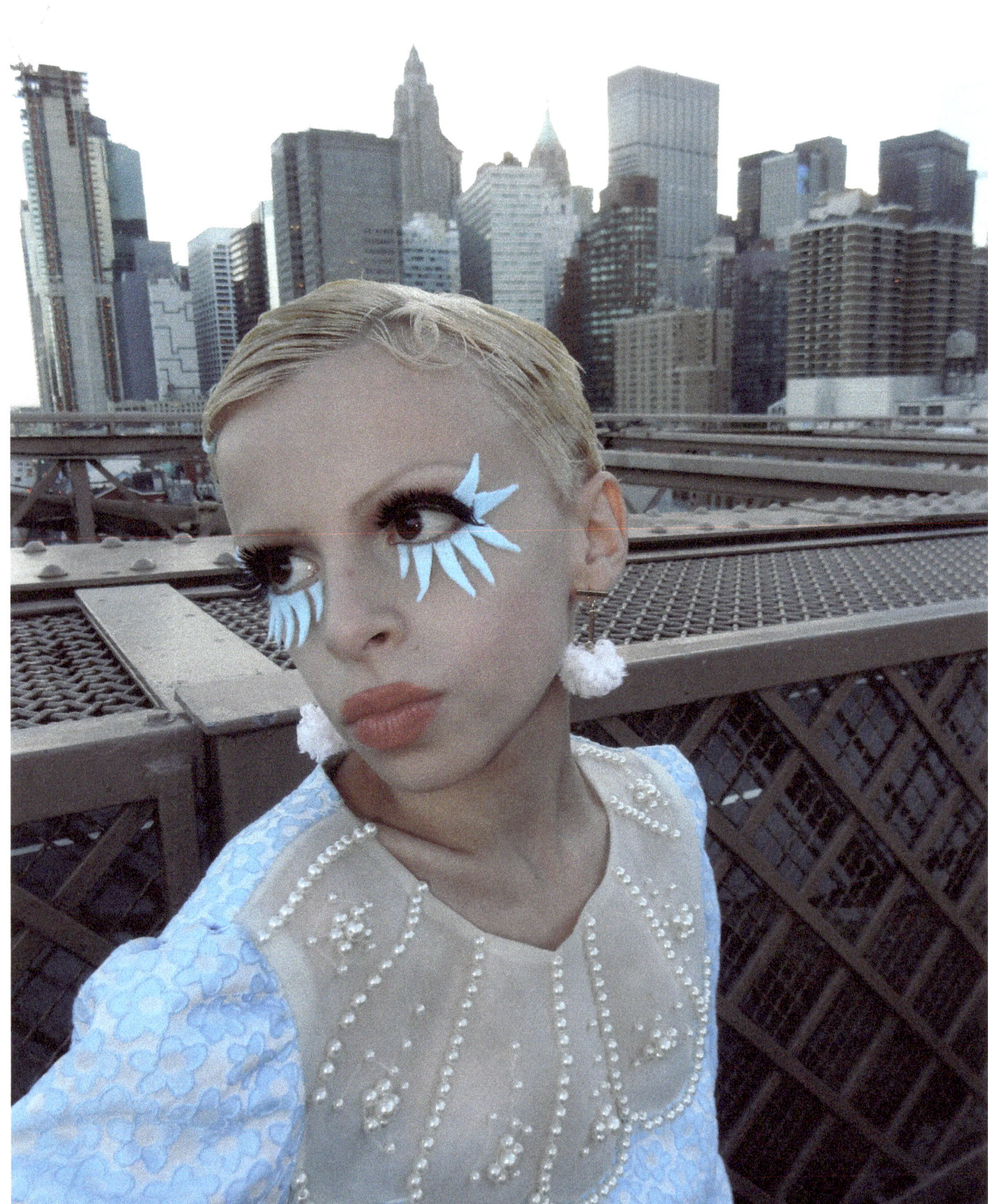

I discovered *RuPaul's Drag Race* before I went to kindergarten. I said, "I want to do that!" I used random items around the house to create "drag" outfits. I used bed sheets, towels, cardboard, paper, ribbon, old shirts, curtains, etc. Now, I am still creating art fashion out of unique materials. I've made a dress, coat, and hat—all out of bubble wrap! I've used a tube top as a skirt and mesh ribbon as a necklace. For this photo, I cut pieces of craft felt into triangles and applied them under my eyes to create a brand new, modern accessory to go with my outfit.

I believe there is no wrong way to do drag. It is an art you can't put limits on. It goes beyond boundaries such as age, race, gender, identity, orientation, status, abilities, or disabilities. I feel best in drag when wearing bright colors and creating from unique items. For me, anything has the potential to be a really fab outfit. I've done "drag creature" outfits inspired by horror films and Hello Kitty. Never let anyone limit what you want to wear and always have fun! I have a blast watching people's reactions to me walking down the street. If what you're wearing doesn't make you smile, it's not fashion. If it doesn't make others smile too, it's not good fashion.

DESMOND NAPOLES (stage name: Desmond is Amazing) is a 12-year-old drag kid and LGBTQ+ advocate.

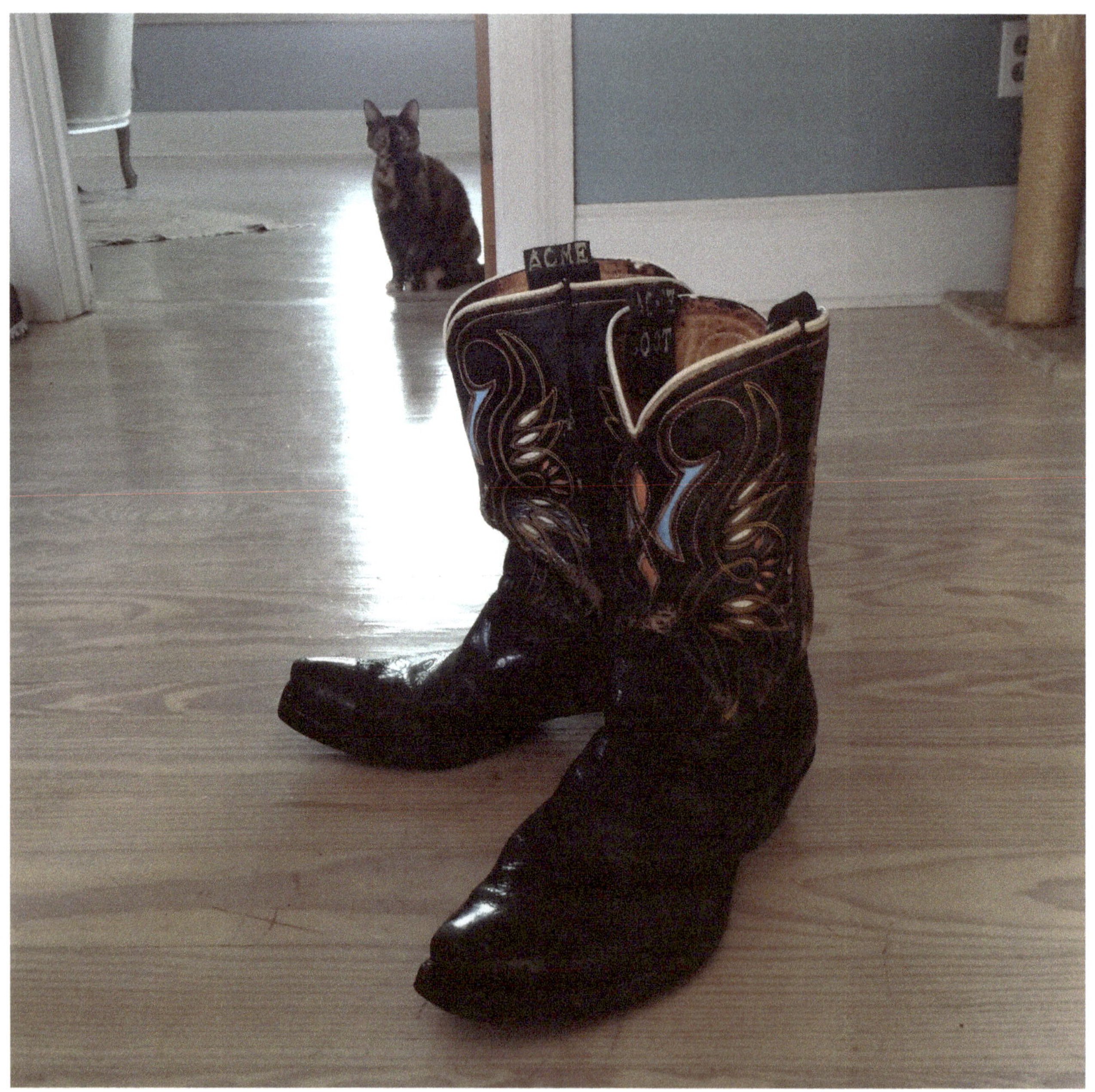

Early childhood is like a blackout drunk. When it's over, people (you know who) get a lot of mileage out of telling you about the awful or charming but always *hilarious* things you did, filling you in on actions, events, and places you don't have any memory of at all—and you have to sit there, trying to look amused. So, for instance, I hear I was a shy child: when strangers approached, I liked to cover my face with my skirt. Really? I didn't wear dresses again until I was in my 40s and fairly sure I had that tendency ("I don't remember!") under control. Another anecdote involved the pair of cowboy boots I had when I was three: there's a picture, somewhere, of me wearing them and nothing else. (But it was Los Angeles . . .) I heard I had some trouble caused by those needle-sharp black leather shit-kickers, maybe ingrown toenails? Something actually painful: so they got thrown away. And I marched to the trash can, dug them out, and put them back on: because what mattered was how I looked not how I felt? Or because I already understood that how you look can transform the way you feel, and knew that making a statement is a way of making room in the world. And yes, cowboy boots cite a story of colonization, genocide, and domination of other species—but I didn't know that when my love of the look began, when boots with the word "boy" in 'em ("made for walking," as the song says) became part of the complex story of being a "girl." I bought cowboy boots—green lizard—with the advance from my first book, and wore them to *shreds*. In the funky elegance of their materials and graceful swirls of their stitching they were all about tough beauty, and the salesman was right: they were cool in summer and warm in winter and you could—I tested this—sleep in them if, too drunk to undress, you passed out.

LAURA MULLEN is the author of eight books and the translator of Veronique Pittolo's *Hero* (Black Square Editions, 2019). She lives in New Orleans.

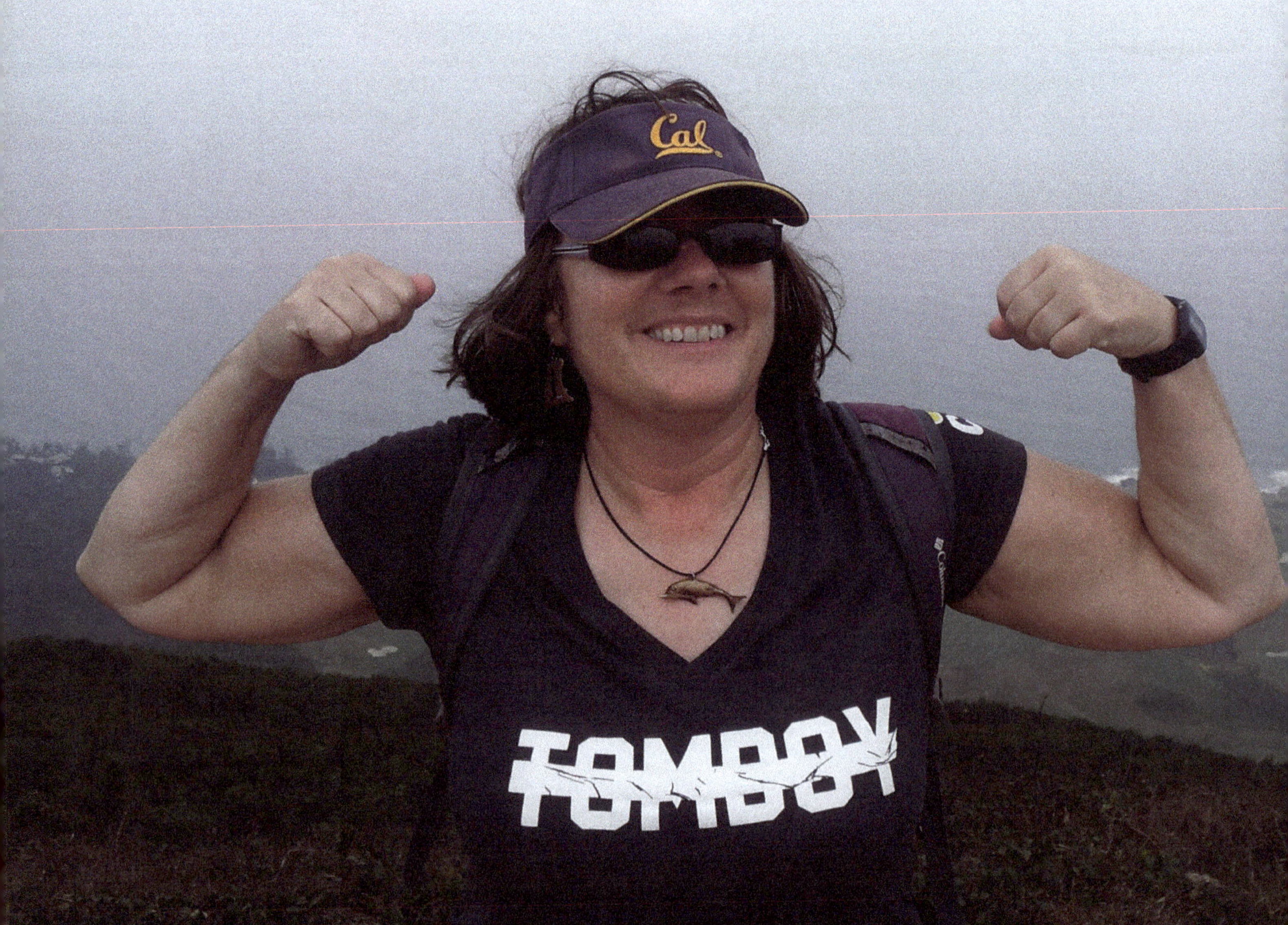

Cal
TOMBOY

This is a photograph taken atop Dragon's Back Trail above Hong Kong, China, in 2019 when I was teaching women's history aboard the Semester at Sea global college program. I felt heroically buff and strong at this moment of pose, having just completed the most challenging hike of my life in China's Yellow Mountains, ascending Mt. Huangshan with its notorious one hundred fifty flights of stone steps. Choosing to be "out" in homophobic China, in sly shirts hinting at my Amazon sensibility, was a choice I made: to be myself as I traveled around the world. Indeed, I went from China and Hong Kong to several other countries where homosexuality was illegal, punishable with prison or even death.

Out since my late teens, I have kept a written record of my dyke life; it is difficult to determine any fine line between the dyke and the writer. My first love letter to a woman (my babysitter: I was seven) shows us posing in bathing suits on a California beach. That casual, "outdoor" clothing style is certainly my signature, for while I was never a *real* tomboy (preferring books about girls to playing sports with girls), I eschewed girly clothing for yes, plaid flannel, cowboy boots, surfing shorts, and in general campout gear, which prepared me well for an adult lifetime at women's music festivals, taking notes.

BONNIE MORRIS is a women's history professor and the author of 17 award-nominated books, including *The Feminist Revolution*, *Sappho's Bar and Grill*, *The Disappearing L*, and *Women's History for Beginners*. Out and proud since age eighteen, she has been a lesbian activist for almost forty years and organized the first-ever exhibit of lesbian musicians in the Library of Congress.

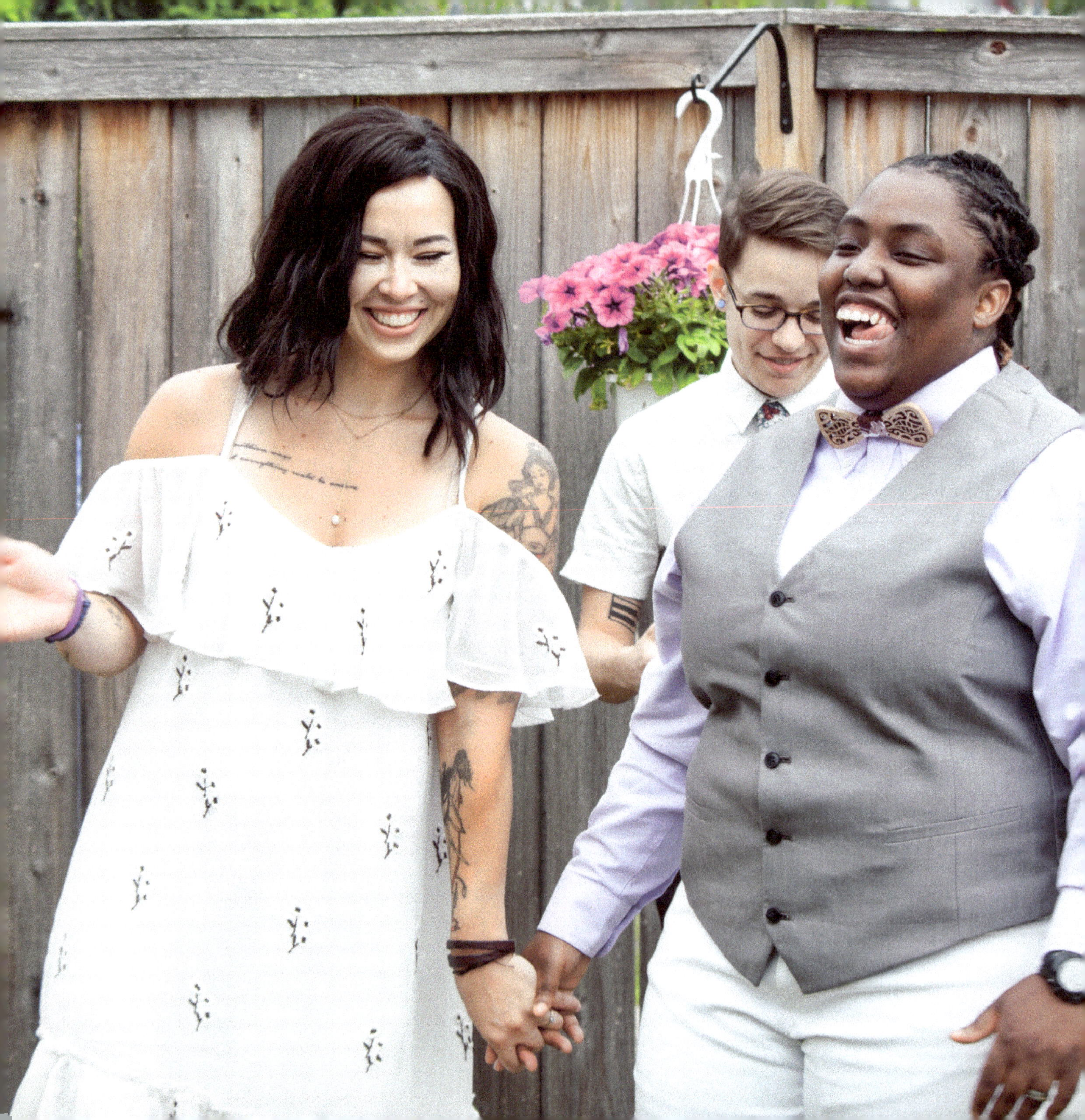

This picture—even with my weird, half-waving, blurry hand—is one of my all-time favorite pictures featuring myself. There're a couple of reasons for this.

The first, and perhaps most obvious, is that this picture was taken right after my partner and I exchanged vows—right after we had our "first kiss" as a married couple. I was elated. In awe. Amazed that I had not only found someone who gets me like Phill gets me, but also at the fact that they actually *wanted* to spend the rest of their life with me. Full of love and short on cash, we rented an Airbnb and got married in the back yard, in front of our closest friends and family. My heart burst with joy the entire day.

The second reason I love this picture is that it is peak *me*—sartorially speaking, that is.

When I came out in 2010 (late bloomer, I know), I didn't know how to dress. I mean, how was I going to pick up chicks if no one thinks "gay" when they look at me? (Seriously, though, I will punch the next cis-het dude who tells me I'm "too pretty to be gay.") I've always had a touch of tomboy to me, so I decided to lean into that and go full baby dyke. You know the type. Sports bra, fitted yet slouchy jeans, high top sneakers, and the cherry on top of my dyke sundae: a beanie.

But it never felt quite right. I don't remember exactly when or how the shift happened, but somewhere along the way, I began to realize that I could have sex with women *and also* be femmey. I can wear makeup, curl my hair, shave my legs, wear dresses—and keep my gay card.

What you see in this picture, then, is a snapshot of me and my queer fashion: happily embracing my femme side, but completely unbothered by the dyke in me who forgot to take the purple hair tie off my wrist and didn't bother to buy a strapless bra before my wedding.

RENÉE MITCHELL-MATSUYAMA is a writer who also works as a student services administrator at the Johns Hopkins School of Nursing. Originally from California, she has also spent significant time in Washington, Wisconsin, and Minnesota. If it weren't for Midwestern winters, Minneapolis would be her favorite city. Renée holds degrees in English and Higher Education Administration from the University of Wisconsin-Madison and is currently pursuing an M.A. in Writing from Johns Hopkins University. She lives in Baltimore, Maryland, with her wife and their two cats.

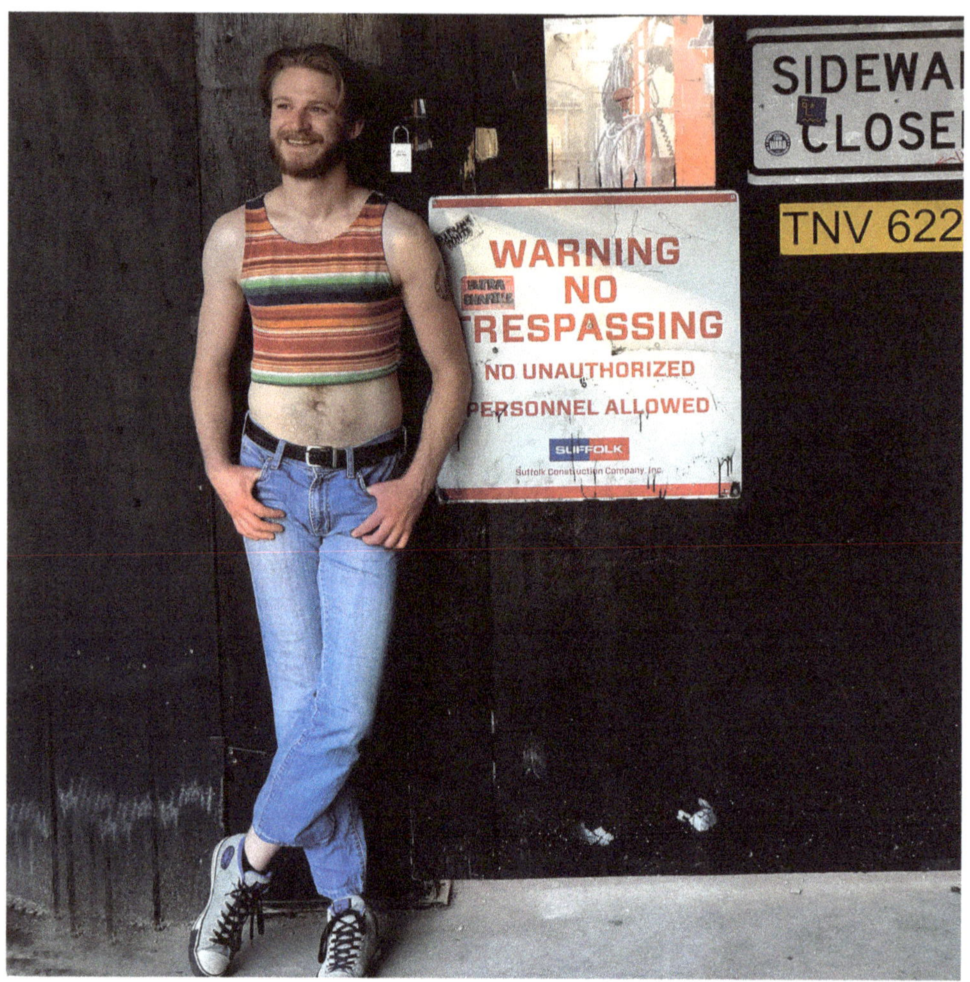

MICHEL MIRABELLA lives in Boston, MA. They identify as non-binary and have been exploring self-expression through fashion and make-up for the last eighteen months. Being more honest and open about themself in how they present to the world has been such a liberating feeling, and they've loved exploring how one article of clothing can express so many different things depending on what it's paired with. Exploring their feminine side through fashion has really transformed their life and how they feel about themself.

THANKS, MR. BOOMER

Why thank you, Mr. Boomer,
For I'm sure you were complimenting my outfit
As you practiced your laser vision on me.
I'm sure you had nothing but nice things to say, and that's why your wife
And friends are also now staring.

I really like my crop top, too.
The way
It hugs the body I've worked for
And doesn't hang baggy off my thin frame.
The way
It makes me stand up just a bit straighter and adds
A flare of strut to my step.
The way
I feel my brain exhale, at home in my body, even if it never finds
A final destination.
The way
It makes me feel like me.

I like your hat, Mr. Boomer.
The way
Its pinched, crumpled complexion matches your facial expression,
And the way it so readily reminds me that you're
"The Greatest Generation."
But Mr. Boomer,
Didn't you fight for my right
To express myself?

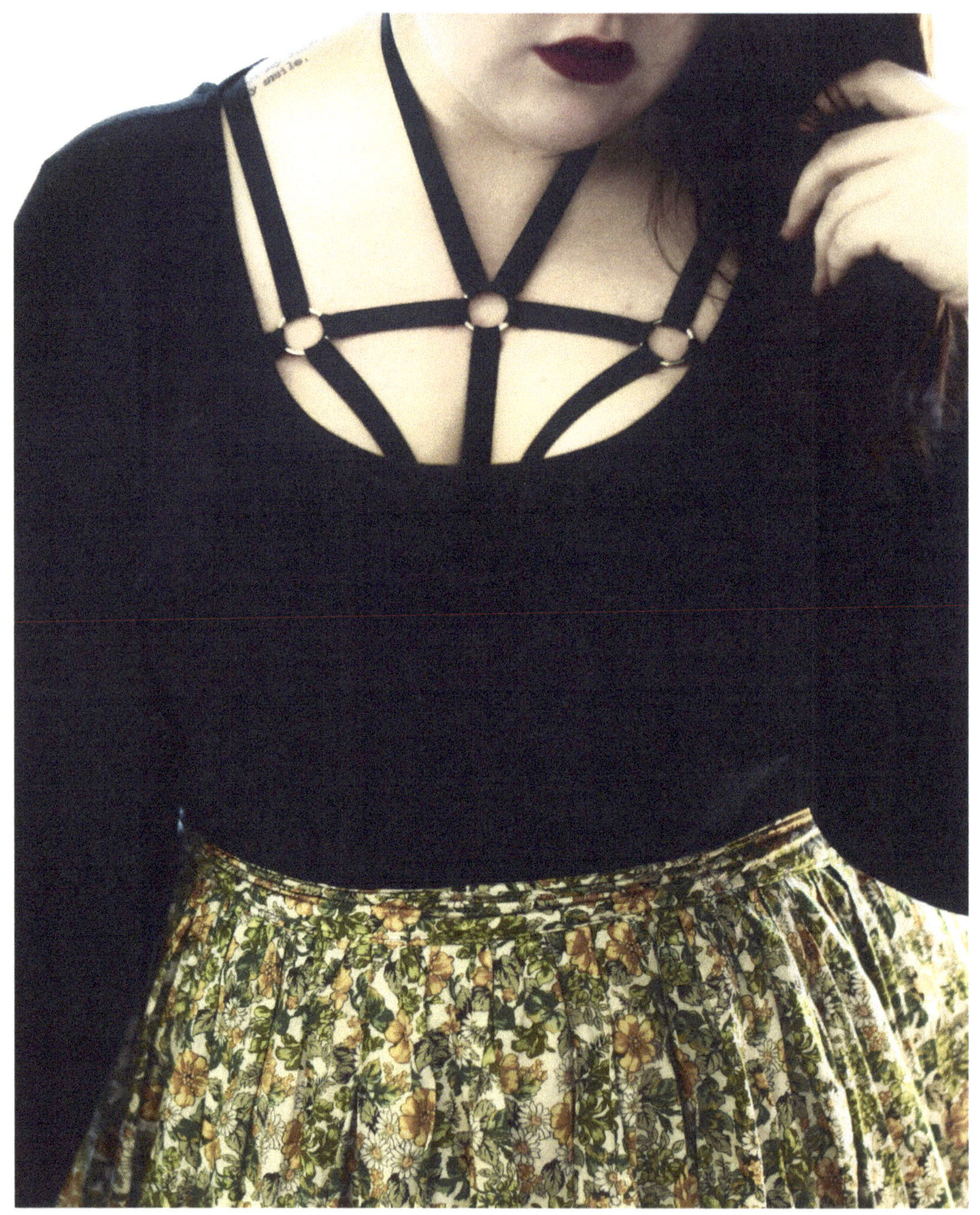

I have no idea how many identities I tried to fit into when I was younger. Ones that were pre-made and pre-approved. Ones that made me easily digestible to the world. Ones that made me quiet. Pretty. Straight. I turned myself into a doll and let society play dress up with me. But, this simple harness bra changed all of that.

Instead of putting clothing on top of who I was, wearing this harness felt like opening my chest up and bringing light to something internal. I was immediately inspired to write the following poem and even though I have evolved and lately overalls feel like magic and I'm all about these ripped up jeans and this knit crop top combo that makes me feel like Kelly Bundy, this harness bra taught me what it felt like to start building my own identity, and it taught me that identity had very little to do with the woman everyone expected me to be.

My identity was a little wild and still timid, but it ceased to be about playing a role. I learned that when I choose femininity from a place of power, instead of having it forced on me, and when I honor the parts of myself that do not align with expectations of femininity, the darkness, the complex sexuality, the hardness, the propensity to demand the world bend to me instead of constantly bending to it—that is when the whole of me becomes tangible. That is when I stop being a doll dressed up like a woman and start being real.

The juxtaposition of me
is something like two jagged incomplete pieces
Shifting and grating against each other in restless, aching discord

Then
sometimes,
when the wind is right and the planetary globs of my organs align,
the angry halves settle into a slow and thrumming movement.

Dynamic and intricate.

And pain and joy and shame and brilliance,
the devious and the pristine acts of my humanity,
come hawking up out of my throat

And

I can breathe.

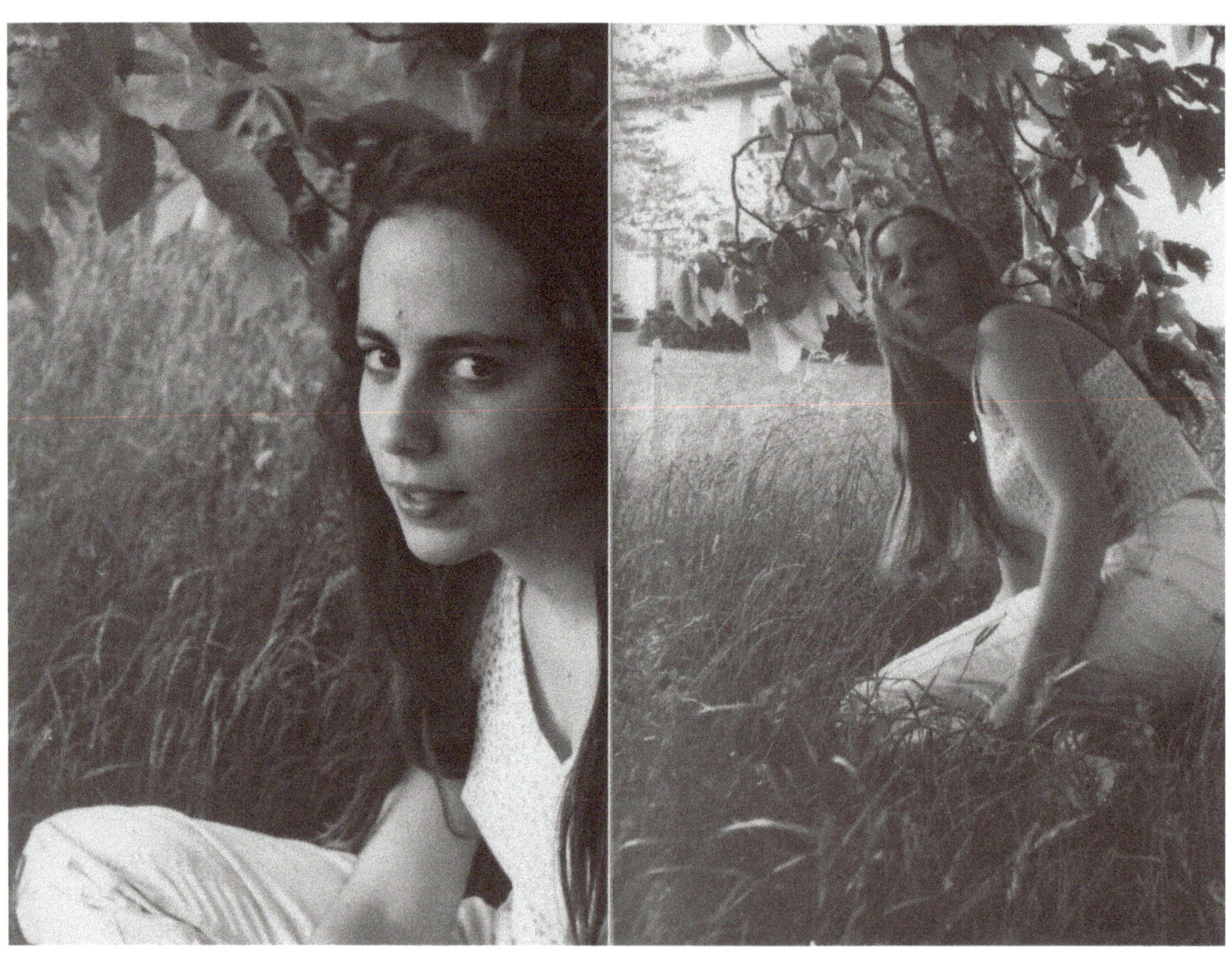

FRUITS

I don't suppose she's read Wu Tsao.
She must be half my age, and yet, with those
fine Chinese eyes, she climbs inside
my eyes as if she knows me, confident
that I, at least, accept her rainbow pride
and dykey style. I do, young one, as
kneeling to bag my apples from a lower bin,
I feel her sink her city gaze into
my tank-top's low-cut top.

heavy hay, soaked dirt
dig potatoes then
catch ride back to town

cut-glass disco beat
strobe-lit
blue-jeaned balls

torch on her tank top
naked muscles,
green eyes

trembling cherry, kiwi,
blushing mango
shake it all down

October sky
distant Andromeda
clean sheets on our cold bed

la lune almost full
gauzy clouds
in my window

Angus head
half-cow, half-bear
black as your lover's hair

black cows in the night
awake by the creek
mist rolling in the valley

MARY MERIAM co-founded Headmistress Press and edits the *Lavender Review: Lesbian Poetry and Art*. She is the author of *My Girl's Green Jacket* (2018) and *The Lillian Trilogy* (2015), both from Headmistress Press. Her poems appear recently in *Poetry*, *Prelude*, and *Subtropics*.

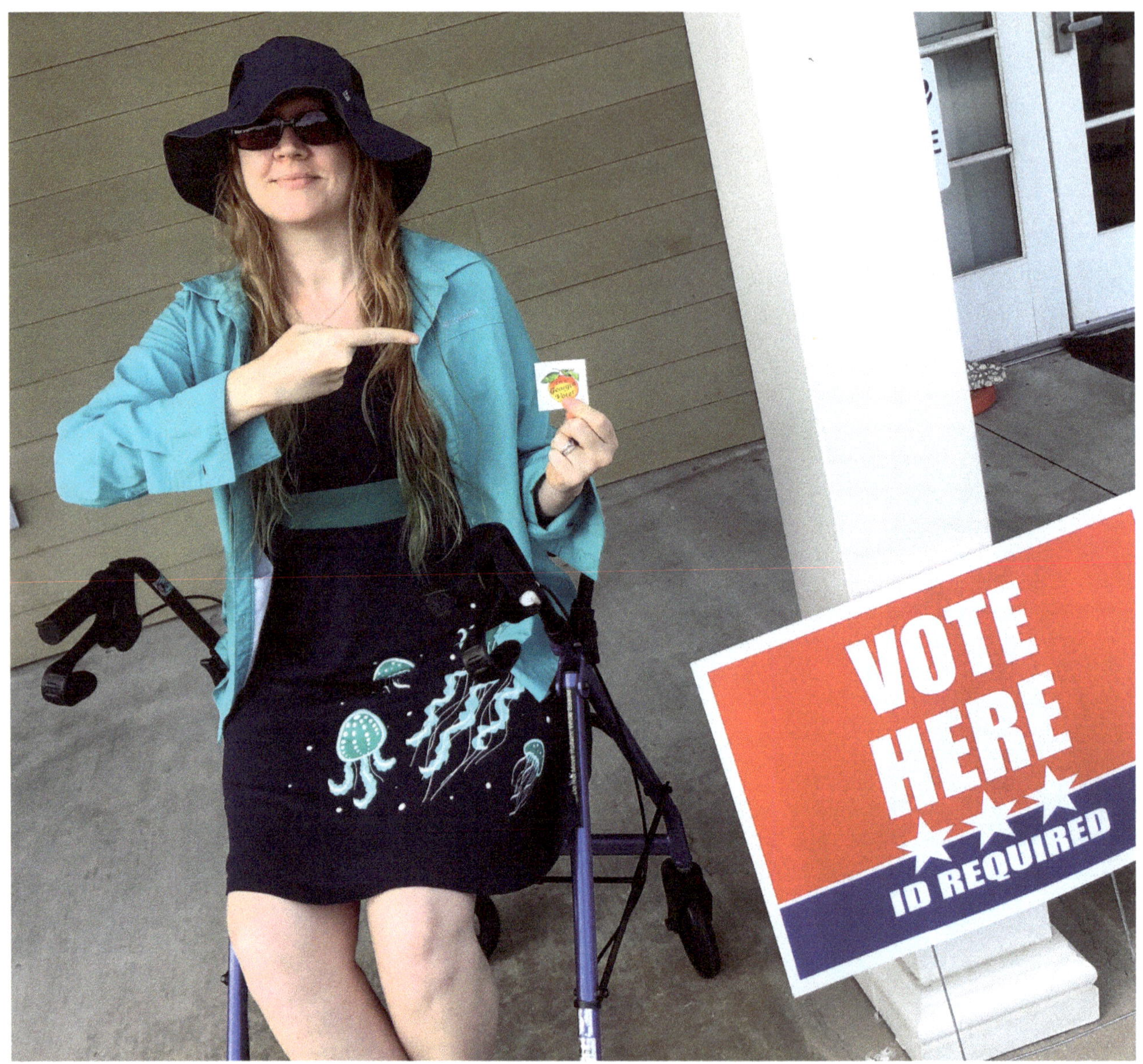

JESSICA MELILLI-HAND'S work appears in the *Carolina Quarterly*, *CALYX*, *Redactions: Poetry & Poetics*, *Hunger Mountain*, *Painted Bride Quarterly*, *Barrow Street*, and the *Minnesota Review*, among others. She won first place in the Agnes Scott Poetry Competition three times: when judged by Terrance Hayes, when judged by Arda Collins, and when judged by Martín Espada. She is an assistant professor of English at the College of Coastal Georgia.

POLL: BEST FEATURE OF THIS DRESS?

- One word: POCKETS

- Svaha's tagline: "removing the gendered equation from clothes"

- Glow-in-the-dark jellyfish!

- The 100% organic cotton doesn't feel like fire the way many clothes feel because an electrical injury frazzled my nervous system into CRPS/RSD, a chronic condition rated more painful than digit amputation without anesthesia except if the digits regrew instantaneously to be amputated again, à la Prometheus's liver and the eagle, but slightly different, and my wife bought this soft-glow-against-the-darkness to cheer me up after we found out that my crushing headaches and pain from sounds and lights (hence my ever-present hat and migra-glasses), my constant nausea and intermittent difficulty walking, and my increased heart arrhythmias and exhaustion were *not* all side effects of the sea-snail-venom-derived medication being continuously pumped into my spine (where neurosurgeons had drilled a hole for a catheter connected to a three-pound titanium pump they had severed my abdominal muscles from skin to implant), no, these were *actually* symptoms of cerebrospinal fluid leaking from my tough-mother dura, but because this dress is so soft and easy to get on and off, it's perfect for all the times after they drain blood from my arm to inject into my spine to try to patch the hole then try again when it doesn't hold then try again but with added glue that may or may not contain bovine (it's a good thing I didn't know ahead of time so I didn't wrestle with this vegetarian dilemma while I didn't have enough CSF cushioning my brain to help me think) and now we *think* the hole is third time's a charm but my brain doesn't know so now it's over-producing CSF and basically giving itself a concussion but slightly different so now I have mal de debarquement syndrome (a fancy French way to say OMG everything is a boat my body is a boat the floor the grass the bed is a boat) but this dress makes me look more merry than miserable as I #cripthevote as I work it grrl at work as I stagger it's a staggering dress get it it's a statement fashioned by medical necessity it has so much to say

- Tumble dry low

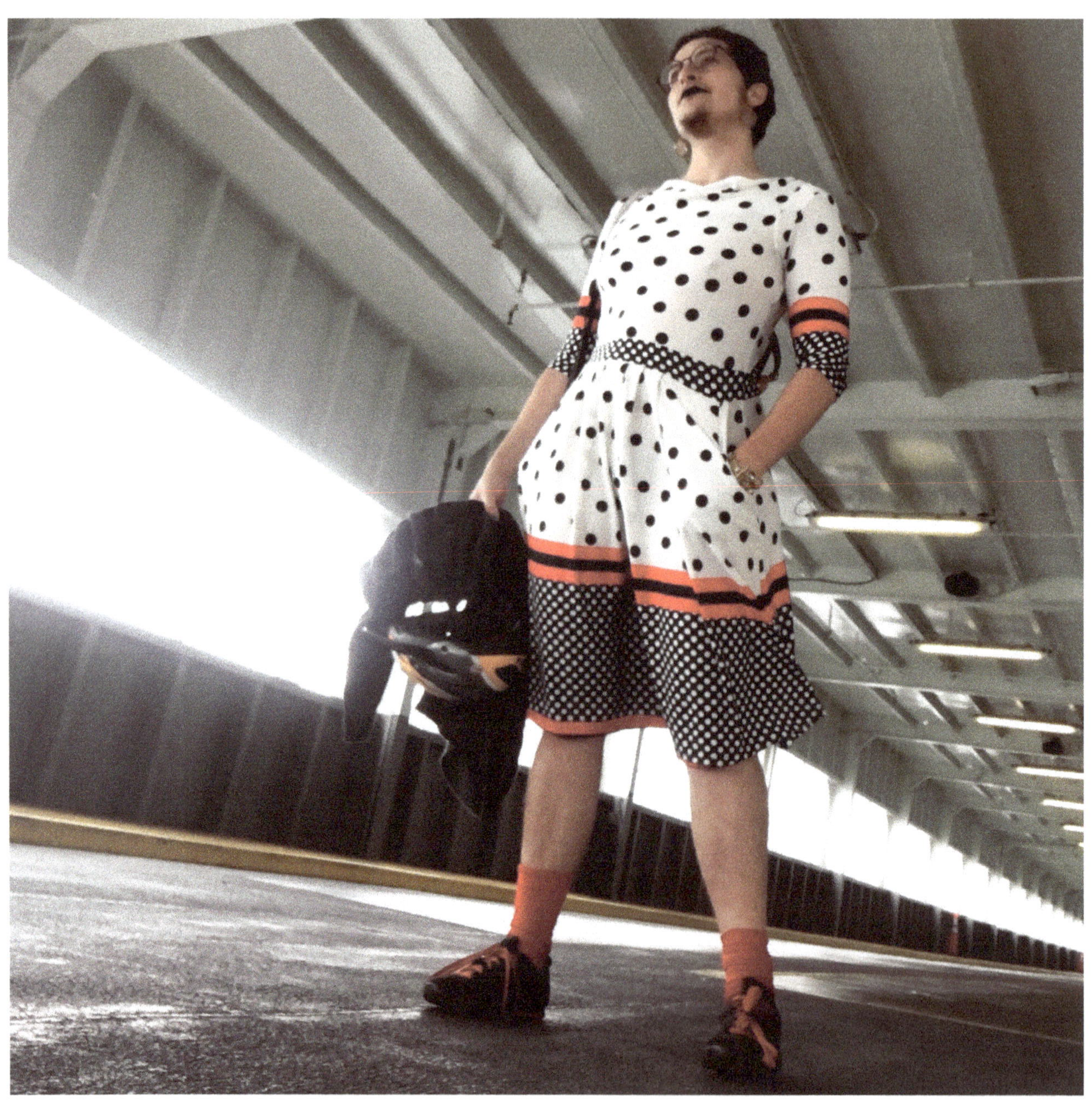

SHOES

Just bought a new pair of shoes. They're corvette red and patent leather. At 5 inches tall, the cursive on the label inside reads "Pleaser." Every time I put them on, my dick stiffens and grows red to match them.

The shoes I wear most often are all scuffed and creased. The once oxblood leather ripples and bulges in the places my ankles have been bending against for five years. The insides of my Dr. Martens are smelly, lined with lint, and increasingly cavernous. The soles have slowly fallen from tromping through alleyways in Guangzhou and New York and learning to walk heavy "like a man." The tread on the yellowy gel-rubber soles has been worn flat from repeated walks between downtown Oakland and Temescal Alley, where I got my first shave. When I first slipped my feet into them, I thought they were girl feet.

Bought the shoes I'm wearing right now from the children's section at REI. They're pink and blue Velcro-strapped sandals with bands of color running along the sides. I bought them on sale. It's less than a month, but the foam footpads already remember the contours of my feet. Slabs of cushy give already bowed from the force of my pronation. The sales clerk asked skeptically, "Are you sure?" I'm never sure, but I do know how small my feet are.

Yesterday's shoes were black with orange accents and laces. They look like normal sneakers. Each of them though, has a metal anchor screwed to the bottom so I can latch them into my bike pedals for better control. I'm still learning how to uncouple my feet from the joints. I've fallen once already (like so much pollen). The bruise on my hip has taken until this morning to fully bloom. These shoes are teaching me contusion and continue.

In middle school I ruined my ankles with a pair of off-brand platform sneakers. The soles fell unevenly. Both my feet tilted in the same direction. I walked off kilter for two years.

I've always hated flip-flops. I will only wear them under duress.

WRYLY T. McCUTCHEN is a hybrid writer, interdisciplinary performer, community educator, and 2018 Lambda Poetry Fellow. Their work has appeared in *Foglifter*, *Tiferet Journal*, and *Nat. Brut*. They hold an MFA from Antioch University. *My Ugly and Other Love Snarls* (University of Hell Press) is their debut poetry collection. Their first memoir is in progress.

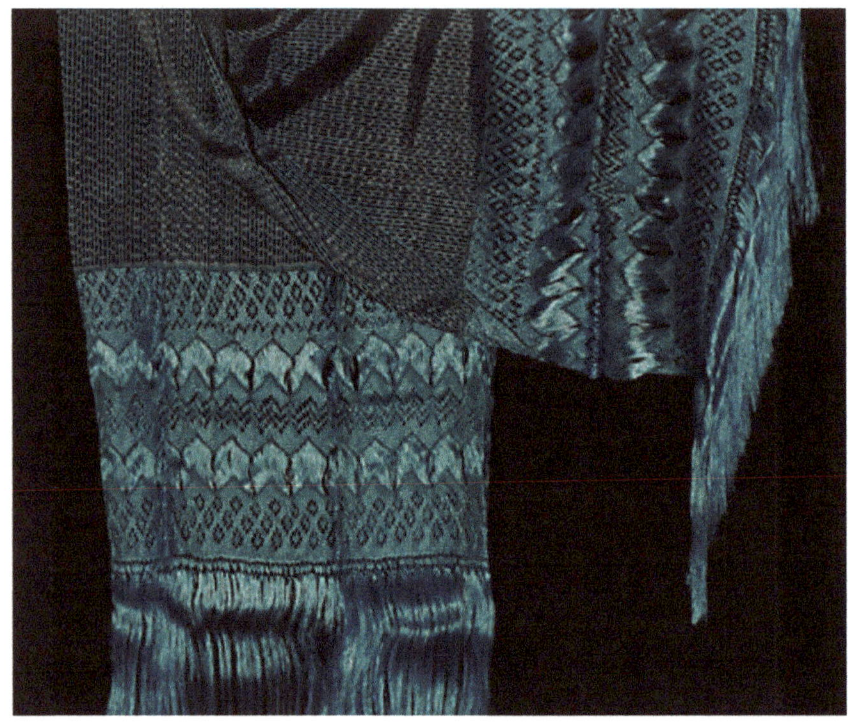

PABLO MIGUEL MARTÍNEZ'S collection, *Brazos, Carry Me* (Kórima Press), received the 2013 PEN Southwest Book Award for Poetry. His chapbook, *Cuent@*, was published by Finishing Line Press in February 2016. Pablo's work has appeared in numerous magazines, journals, and anthologies, including *Borderlands: Texas Poetry Review, Gay and Lesbian Review, Pilgrimage,* and *This Assignment Is So Gay: LGBTIQ Poets on the Art of Teaching.* His literary work has received support from the Artist Foundation of San Antonio, the Alfredo Cisneros Del Moral Foundation, and the National Association of Latino Arts and Culture. Pablo is a Co-Founder of CantoMundo, a national retreat-workshop for Latinx poets.

EL REBOZO

Soon after my mother died, my sister and I went through Mamá's personal effects. Our family occupied that narrow, creaky space between solidly middle-class and precariously middle-class, which meant Mamá left few things of bankable value. But one intangible she bequeathed to us was her sense of style.

Everyone in Mamá's family, women and men, was invariably stylish. Her father was a projectionist at the Aztec Theater here in San Antonio. Consequently, Mamá, her sister, and her mother were avid film buffs. They followed the stars of Mexico's golden age of cinema and emulated their signature glamor—through a budget-conscious version. Stars such as María Félix and Dolores Del Río were their icons. One of the items of clothing those stars wore on and off screen is the rebozo, a uniquely Mexican garment that is much more than 'shawl,' its English-language translation, suggests.

A rebozo, regardless of the textile from which it's made, is a birth-to-death accessory (mothers use it to wrap and carry babies; it was also used by indigenous women as a death shroud), so it is highly prized. My mother's rebozo, given to her by her mother, my Abuela Beatriz, is a stunningly beautiful example of rebozo de bolita. It's made of silk that comes in ball-shaped skeins, hence the name. Mamá's rebozo is the color of the turquoise waters of Mexico's Yucatán Peninsula. She wore it only on special occasions. It was wrapped in flimsy tissue paper and kept in its original box.

"It's the only thing I want to remember her by," I said.

"What on earth do you want with it?" My sister grimaced as she asked this. "It's something women wear. I'm keeping it."

I wouldn't dishonor Mamá's memory by arguing with my sister, so I didn't challenge her. A few months after Mamá's death, I made a trip to Mexico. I found a rebozo similar to Mamá's, but couldn't afford it. When I returned to San Antonio, I bought a less elaborate one. Like my identity, rebozos are mestizo, that is, they represent a coming together of Mexico's indigenous cultures and Spanish traditions. The Spanish word rebozo refers to the act of covering or protecting oneself. Every time I wrap myself in my rebozo I am enveloping myself in humility and protecting myself against anyone who might deny or dishonor who I am.

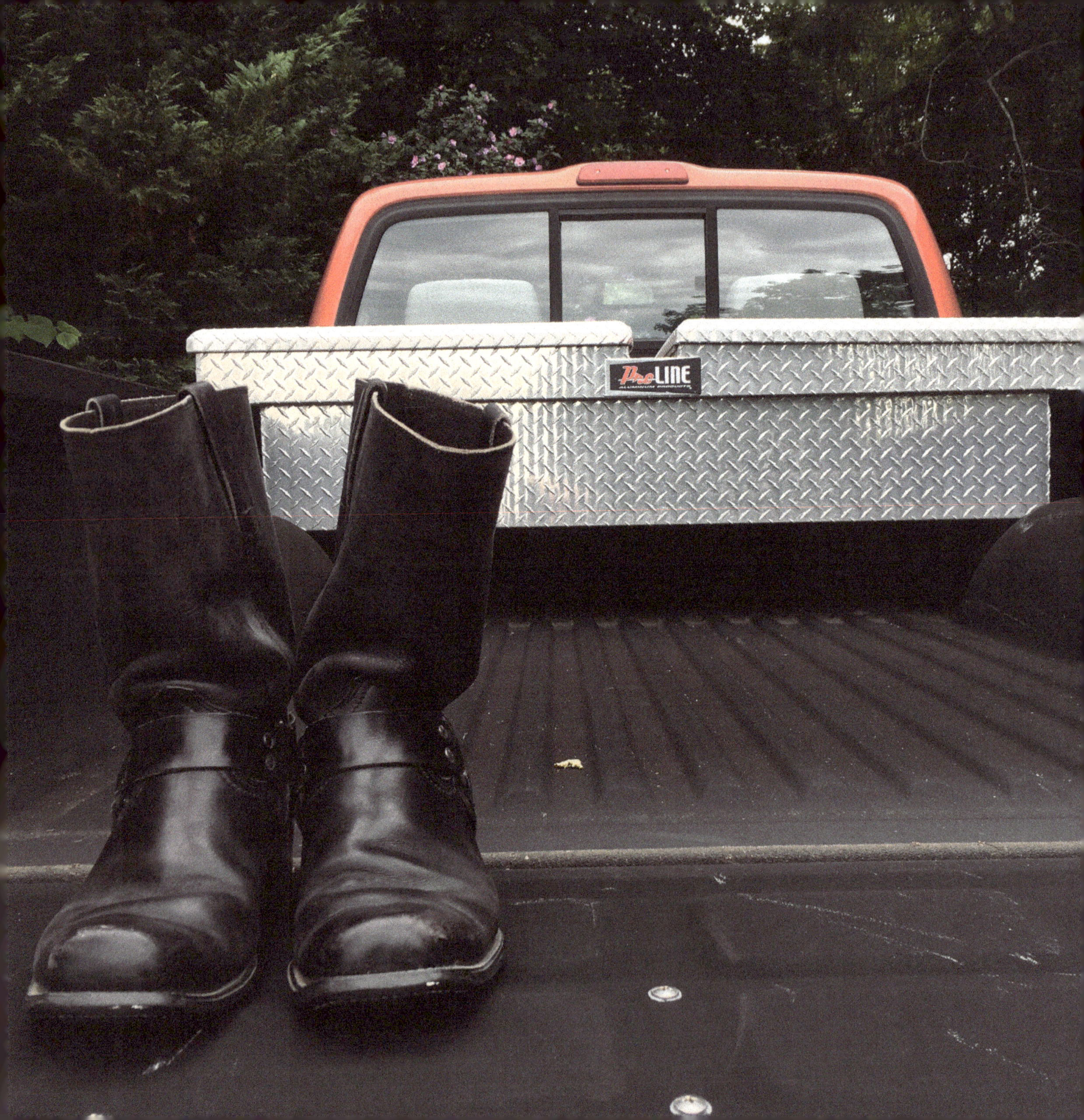

BOOTS

The first man I slept with, a college RA,
mocked them, the grimy work boots I wore.
He found them unfashionable, I suppose,
a marker of my rural West Virginia roots.
The men I grew up around, the men
I began to desire, all wore baseball caps
and boots, footwear built for farm work or
wood-gathering on forested mountain
slopes. I learned to love country boys,
their broad shoulders, fuzzy forearms,
bearded cheeks, the curving density of
their chests, biceps, and buttocks. I wore
what they wore, first to fit in, to belong,
then to adopt some part of their scruffy
toughness, their hairy erotic power,
their defiance, confidence, and strength.
Black biker harness-straps came early, then
a pair of cowboy Dingos my grandmother
bought me for my birthday. Later, deep-tread
Wolverines and Brahma Predators, the kind
my classmates wore during forestry field trips
to Core Arboretum and Coopers Rock.

The Mountaineer Look—first protective
coloration, then, inevitably, personal style,
what these days I jokingly dub Redneck Chic—

who knew how sweetly, seamlessly, my hillbilly
history would translate, sipping Scotch in
my first leather bar, guzzling beer in my first
bear bar? In DC, San Francisco, Chicago,
I found dim gay cosmos where a country boy
might briefly belong, full of flannel shirts,
denim jackets, camo pants, bushy beards,
furry chests, and boots. The same don't-mess-
with-me Ariats, Justins, Carhartts, Timberlands,
Durangos—made for pickup trucks, barnyards,
Appalachian towns like the one I came from,
like the one where I've ended up, those boots
are just right for Pride marches, backroom
frolics, dungeon scenes, just right for

today's shirtless, harnessed, goateed cub
kneeling before me in a corner of
the San Francisco Eagle, servicing the same
black biker harness-straps I've owned
since 1977, buffing the boots
with a cloth before bending down to lap
the decades-scuffed toes, run his young
and reverent tongue over old leather in
spit-shine surrender, while I sigh and smile
and run my father-fingers through his warm
and wiry beard, his wavy chestnut hair.

JEFF MANN has published five books of poetry, *Bones Washed with Wine*, *On the Tongue*, *Ash*, *A Romantic Mann*, and *Rebels*; three collections of essays, *Edge*, *Binding the God*, and *Endangered Species*; a book of poetry and memoir, *Loving Mountains, Loving Men*; six novels, *Fog*, *Purgatory*, *Cub*, *Salvation*, *Country*, and *Insatiable*; and three volumes of short fiction, *A History of Barbed Wire*, *Desire and Devour*, and *Consent*. With Julia Watts, he co-edited *LGBTQ Fiction and Poetry from Appalachia*. The winner of two Lambda Literary Awards and four National Leather Association-International literary awards, he teaches creative writing at Virginia Tech.

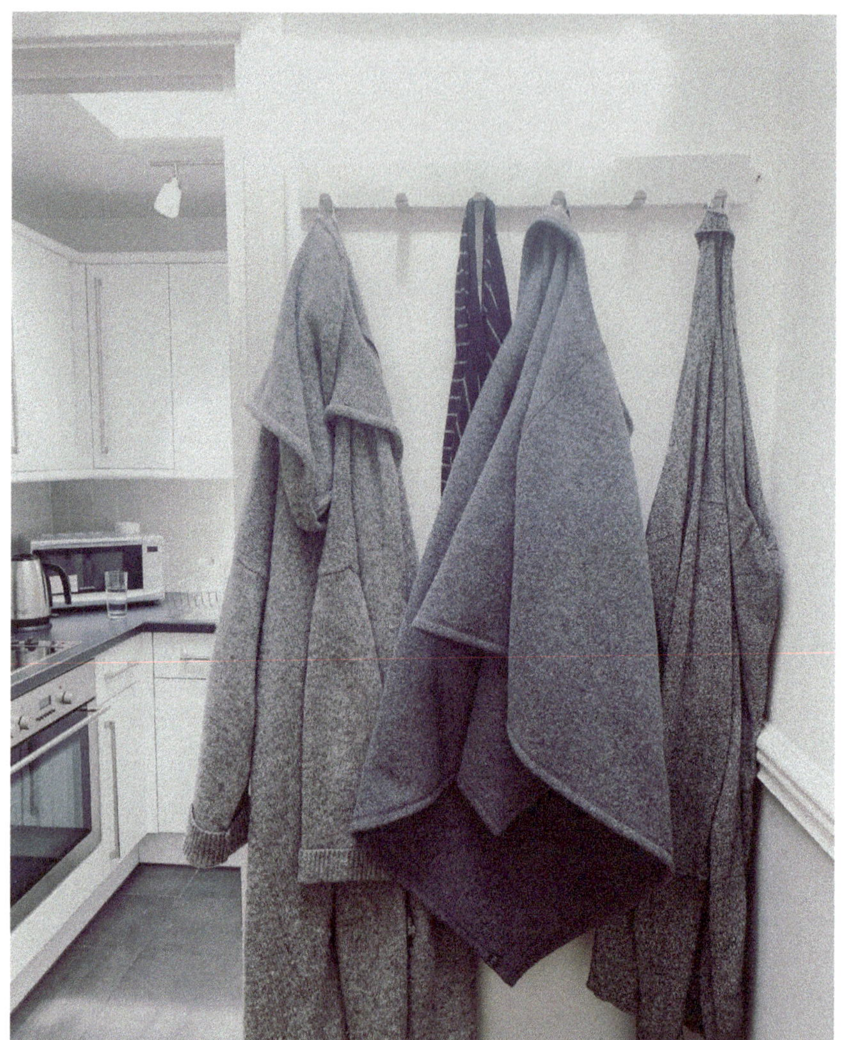

K. ANN MACNEIL lives and works at the top of an island (Manhattan), near the bank of an estuary (where the Harlem and Hudson Rivers meet), at the edge of a two-hundred-acre forest where she and her grown daughter toy with the idea of writing a collection of urban fairy tales. Her work has been published, most recently, in *This Assignment Is So Gay: LGBTIQ Poets on the Art of Teaching; The Still Blue Project: Writing with Working Class Queers in Mind;* and *Love, Always: Partners of Trans People on Intimacy, Challenge, and Resilience.*

DAHLIAS

On your first trip to London, with your other mum and me, in the off-off-season, on the absolute cheap,
you figured out that some book editions weren't available in the States, not even at Bank Street Books,
three neighborhoods south of us, at home in New York, so eight-year-old you squeezed your doll-sized sweaters
into your bright pink canvas purse and rolled your matching bag filled with paperbacks from an Oxfam shop
onto what felt like a cruelly early return flight.

By the same time the next year,
your new backpack, that one pale pink and almost-too-big,
found on super-sale at an L.L. Bean outlet, would be one you would shuttle between
two apartments, albeit in the same building.

A decade-and-some later, after your finals, after an impossible year,
we followed my partner, your improbable step-parent, back to London
using her university-fueled air miles, to present his work
at the Design Museum, at a fancy-sounding symposium.

At the V&A, you remembered a junior-explorer backpack in a disappointing blue,
and a scavenger hunt checklist, where we couldn't talk our way into the exhibit,
so you insisted on a Dior book; we spent an hour in sight of the one dress in their regular collection
before a visit to a nearby Waterstone's, after we learned that the spectral Oxfam shop had closed,
for a jumble of discounted poetry books, as many as you could carry, unsurprisingly, in unfamiliar editions.

We stacked them in size-order, spines aligned, steps from the kitchen with skylights,
a drying rack, Green Fairy dish soap, an electric kettle, and what was left of my clean clothes hung on hooks,
my makeshift closet, in our borrowed fifth floor walk-up, rented with your step-parent's housing stipend:
"I told them I would be traveling with my family," they said, breaking, I suspect, your heart and mine, both.

We stopped near the flat for white dahlias, cut in South Kensington,
wrapped in newsprint as the flower market had closed, the last bunch, at the last minute,
and spooned sugar cubes, brown ones only, into mint tea
that you deemed the best, possibly ever.

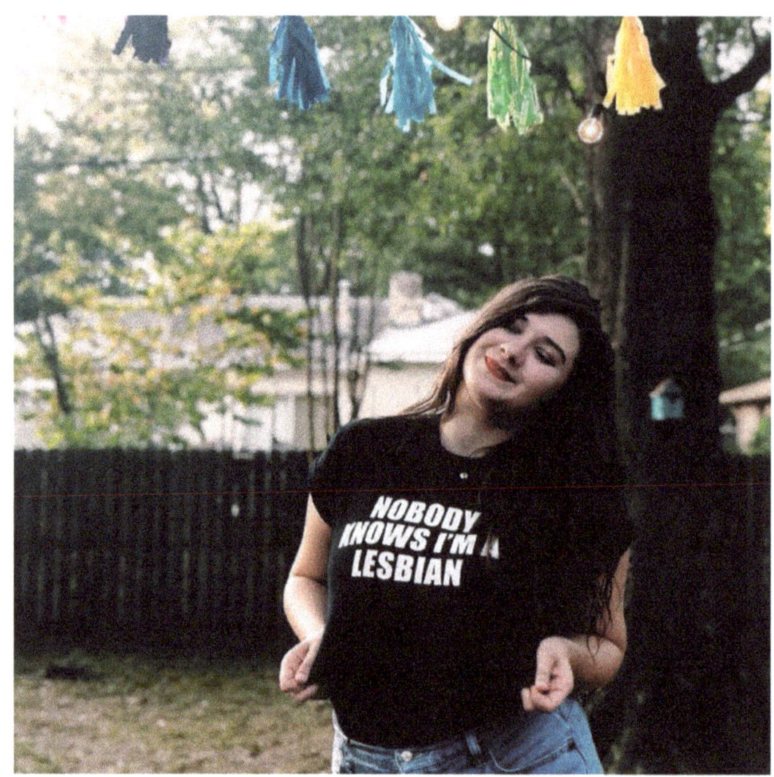

KATHRYN LELAND is a poet from Austin, Texas. She is currently an MFA candidate at the University of Mississippi and holds a B.A. in English–Creative Writing from Hendrix College. She works as an associate editor with Sibling Rivalry Press and reader for *Yalobusha Review*. Her work has appeared in *The Hunger* and *Rust + Moth*, and her debut chapbook, *I Wore The Only Garden I've Ever Grown*, was published in January 2017 with Headmistress Press. She lives in Mississippi with one cat and a collection of half-dead houseplants.

The no-frills version of the story is this: I bought a rad T-shirt one year to wear to Pride, but afterward it made its way into my regular rotation. One day I wore it and made a genuine human connection with someone because of the slogan printed on the chest. Not ten minutes later I flipped that shirt inside out in hopes that I would get better service at a body shop where I needed a minor car repair. It worked, and afterward I had to face up to what I'd done. I'm pretty femme-presenting which, in my case, often means I'm straight-passing. This is a kind of privilege and something I had just abused, not for safety, but for gain.

When I was in undergrad, I had this incredible mentor who taught me that one of the most radical things I can do as a queer person is to be out whenever and wherever I safely can. Her visibility and openness are two of the things that helped me come out and realize that queer adults could be anything they wanted to be (yes, a very elementary school moment). I thought that when I began teaching (like I had that semester), I would be as out as possible for others the way she had been for me, but on that day I wasn't anywhere close.

I don't like the version of myself that ignored my privilege and chose to shed my queerness. When I wear that shirt now I am still that person, but I am also a person who is trying constantly to be better than that. I like me better when I am out.

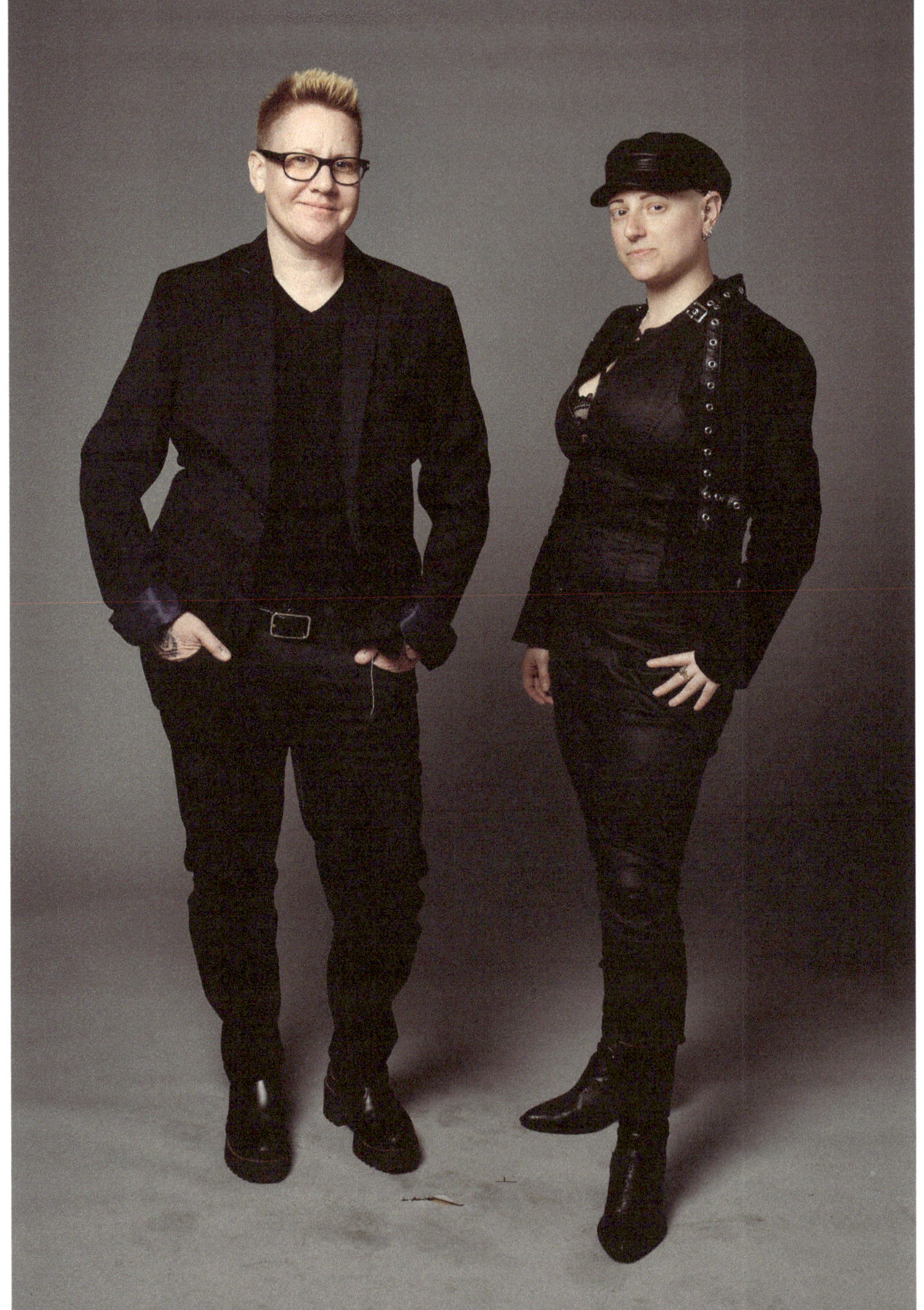

I was always obsessed with jackets. Convinced it was only a matter of being in the right place at the right time with the right amount of money available on my credit card . . . I would find the jacket that finally made me feel . . . like me. I put them all through the same excruciating checklist: Will this jacket give me broader shoulders? Will it give me narrower hips? Will it disguise my D-cup bosoms? It was protection. It was preservation—not just presentation.

In my late 30s, I really started giving myself permission to consciously lean into my masculinity. I started owning my natural walk—still hips with wide legs, my shoulders broad. I wore oxfords and brogues, I cut my hair, I stopped wearing makeup. I started a job that had good health insurance—for the first time in a long time. And with a genetic predisposition to estrogen-fueled cancers, a long history of needing biopsies and MRIs, and never knowing if this would be the time they say the dreaded words, I opted to get a preventative double mastectomy. I had great clarity that I did not want reconstruction of any kind (which took a year of convincing for my surgeon). Until my recovery, there had never been anything in my emotional or psychological vocabulary that had challenged my actual gender as part of my self-expression.

But there I was at forty-five, post-surgery in June 2015, staring at this new body. And I realized that the whole search for that jacket—trying to find something, anything to make me feel more like me—was, maybe, me unconsciously advocating for a gender identity I didn't even know I wanted yet. And I was grateful for something in me, pushing me not to reconstruct, because for me, taking away my breasts ended up giving me everything my life had been missing. This whole time I thought I was a big dyke who was avoiding breast cancer, but little did I know, I was actually a trans masculine, non-binary person who didn't want breasts at all.

LIZ LEIFER is a non-binary/trans masculine Co-Owner of Play Out Apparel.

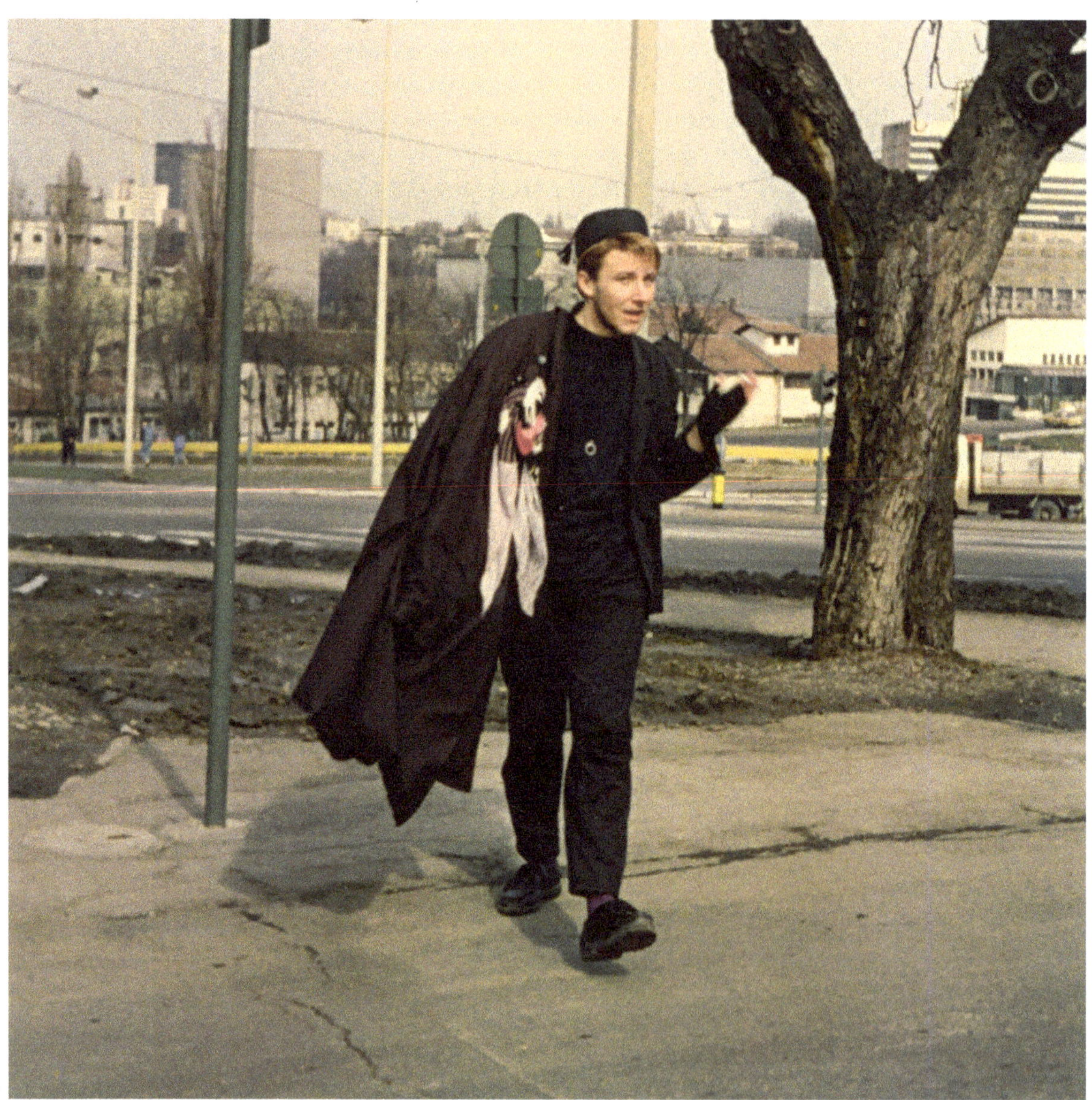

MY FUROSHIKI

There are various unusual items in the picture, such as I do not wear any longer, even though some of them still linger in my wardrobe cabinets. I made the quasi-fez from an old national costume (Serbian from Austrian Militärgrenze—nowadays in Croatia) ethnic cap by covering it in black rayon material and adding to it a dark purple tassel from a luxe New Year gift; also purple knee high socks like the bishops' ones; black suede brogues with thick rubber soles the colour of red-wine-based vinegar; a blouse/sweatshirt and a vest on top of it made from the same black cotton knitwear; and a long black overcoat going all the way down to between the ankles and mid-shins.

And then the viscose furoshiki imprinted with huge faces in the traditional wood-block print style, which I wore as a scarf for several years.

It came from Japan, from my pen pal in Chiba City. She had written to me when I was a first-year student minoring in Japanese at Belgrade University. We exchanged opinions, she helped me improve my written Japanese, and I tried to reciprocate by helping her with her English. At some point, I sent her a pair of handicraft fur slippers, and she sent me a furoshiki and obi netsuke. I cannot describe the uniqueness of that furoshiki at the time (1980s). Even if there were some people who had travelled to Japan and could have had one in Belgrade, it was sure to be with a different pattern and size, made of different material.

I knew it was meant as a wrapper for gifts, but I used it as a scarf—rather daring for a young male in backward, macho Serbia thirty plus years ago—and wore it often to various social occasions, glad when it caught attention.

Unfortunately, it is no longer in my possession: it was stolen from me while travelling in the 1990s. Still, it is in the "closet of my mind," locked with all the precious memories of what should have been material mementos, lost through wear and tear, accident, or theft.

MIODRAG KOJADINOVIC has been wandering around planet Earth for over half a century, trying to make sense of it all and not really succeeding. He writes, takes photos, translates . . . used to teach at universities and work in embassies, for various media, and in NGOs.

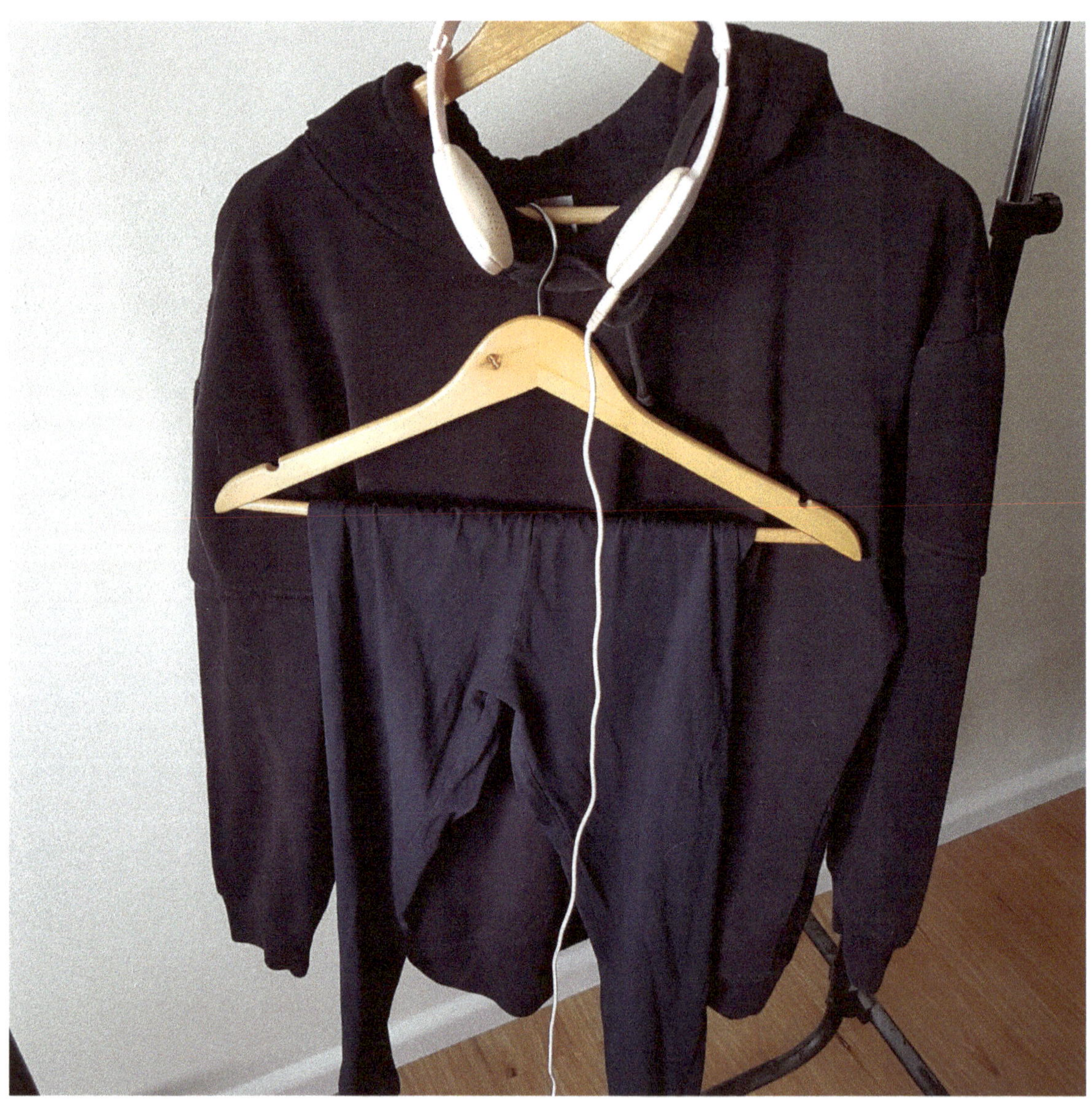

FERRIS KNIGHT is a writer and producer from Melbourne, Australia.

When asked where I'm from, I say Melbourne, Australia. If they press on, Essendon. Even those who don't know the area know it hosts one of the national football teams.

Niddrie, just next door, is a small suburb 8 miles from Melbourne. It was originally inhabited by the Wurundjeri peoples of the Kulin nation. There is about half a mile of shops before the road continues into Essendon, but in the past year many "for lease" signs have gone up. The florist, butcher, hairdresser, baker, and more were all gone.

Autumn in Melbourne is crisp, with winds so strong they almost push you over. This day, however, was calm enough I could still hear the music through my headphones. I threw on what I had lying around to go and get some sushi.

Walking home, there was a man sitting on a skateboard. I'd seen him in the past with his Bible. Upon seeing me, he got up, following me.

"Hey. Hey. How are you?"

"What are you doing?"

I pretend I can't hear him, leaving my headphones on.

"Hey. Stop! I know you can hear me!"

He's so close, nearly touching me now.

"Don't you know, you're supposed to make Niddrie look beautiful!"

I turn quickly into the library, hoping he won't follow me into a public place. He doesn't, and I wonder if he will harass another woman after I leave.

At home I head straight to the shower, trying to wash off this man's words. Rubbing my skin raw, slut-shaming thoughts enter my head—was I not beautiful, or was it by leaving that I was taking it away? Were my leggings too tight? My jumper too short? Was it that I didn't wear make-up? Did I look too gay and like I needed salvation? I don't know how to look less like I want attention.

I didn't want to be beautiful. I just wanted some sushi.

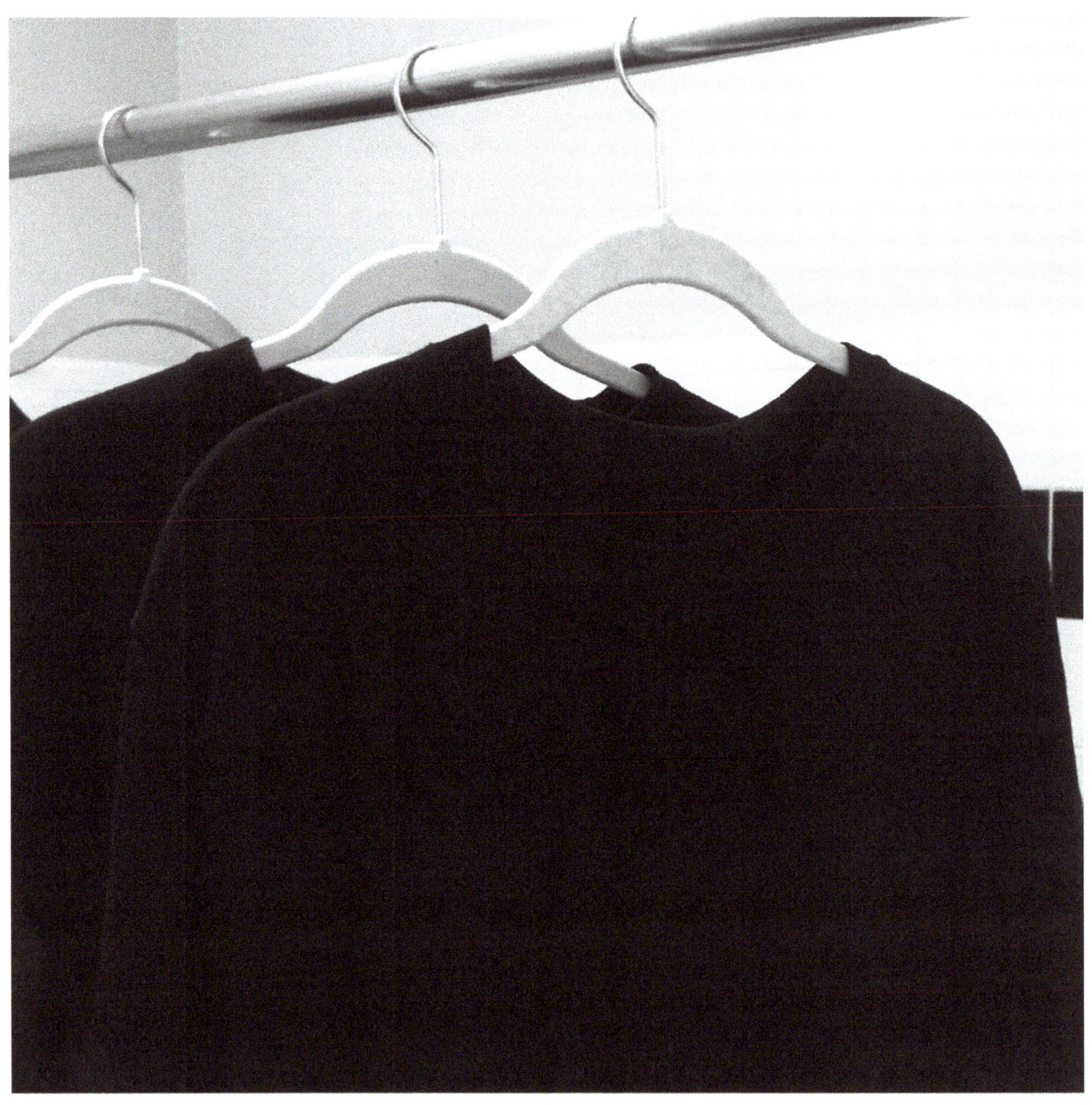

COLLIN KELLEY is a poet, novelist and journalist from Atlanta, Georgia.

THE TIMELESS BLACK T-SHIRT

Don't you know—I always wear black.

-Georgia O'Keefe

I've lost track of how many black t-shirts I've owned over the last thirty-odd years. From overpriced Calvin Klein to cheap Walmart, a plain black t-shirt is not a staple of my wardrobe, it *IS* my wardrobe. I started wearing my "uniform" of black tees and jeans in 1987 when I was still in high school. I never cared about fashion trends, and shopping for clothes was anathema to me. I just wanted to get dressed and get on with my day without having to think about it. A black t-shirt is a classic, minimalist, and functional look that works for all occasions. When I give a reading or attend a social event, I dress up the uniform with a black blazer. Formal events, too. In winter, I add a black sweater or coat. For years, I was told my wardrobe was boring and unimaginative and that I should "add a splash of color." There were times when even I thought of myself as a freak for always wearing the same clothes, but then I discovered that I was in the company of other great artists and leaders. Georgia O'Keefe said her decision to wear black was not preference but practicality: if she started worrying about picking out colors to wear, she would have no time for painting. This was an "ah-ha!" moment for me. I, too, would rather be creating than worrying about clothes. Similar feelings have been expressed by Apple co-founder Steve Jobs (famous for his black turtlenecks and jeans), President Barack Obama (who distilled his White House wardrobe to navy and grey suits) and Albert Einstein (who had a closet full of the same suit). When Sharon Stone infamously wore a black Gap t-shirt to the 1996 Academy Awards ceremony, I felt vindicated. After all these years, I cannot picture myself wearing anything else. It's become a personal trademark. Here's a simple truth: fashion trends come and go, but a black t-shirt is forever. Timeless. Buy yourself a dozen and wear them proudly and often. Or every day.

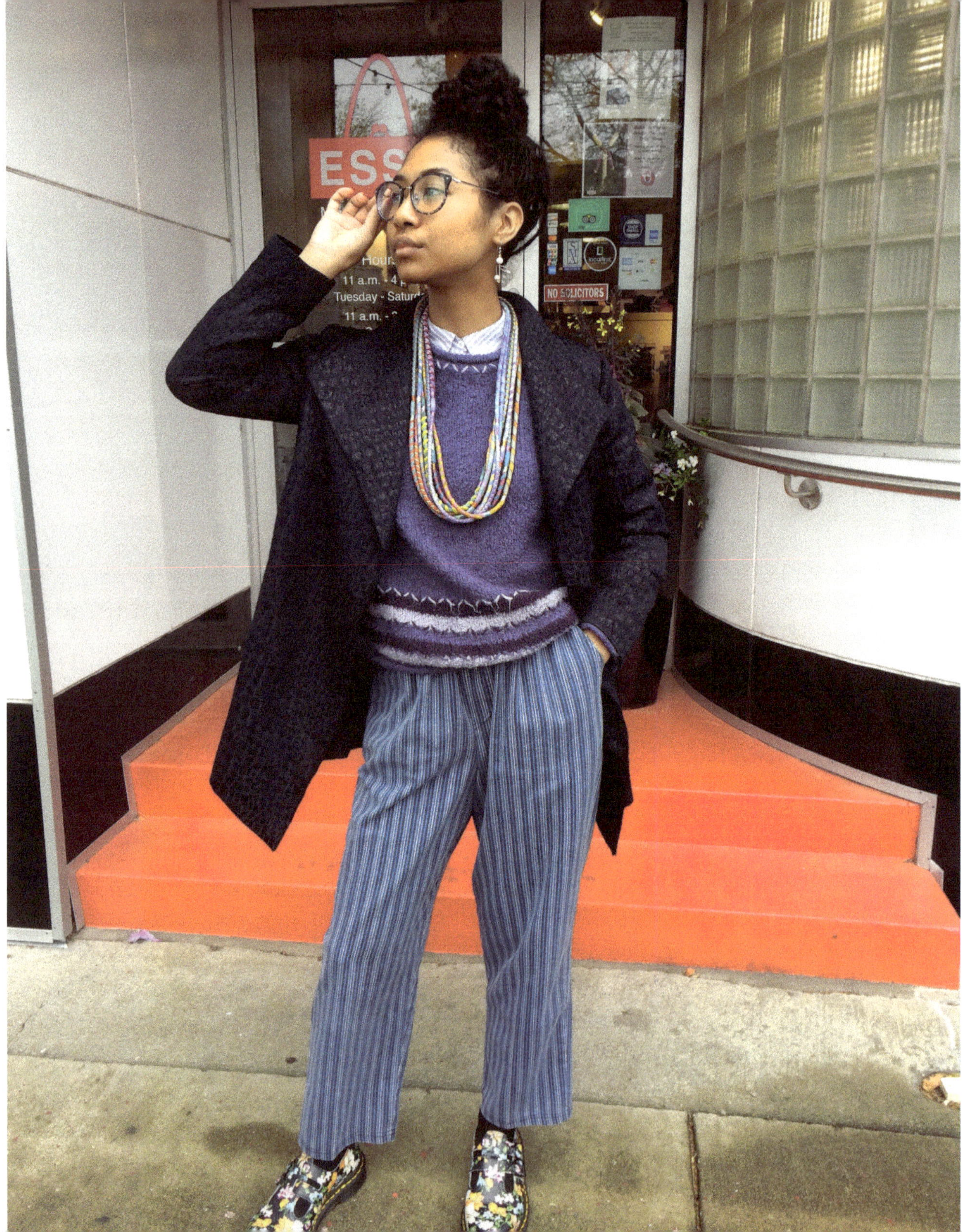

ESS
Hour
11 a.m. - 4
Tuesday - Saturd
11 a.m. -
NO SOLICITORS

As a costumer, I've always been drawn to fabrics as a way to create characters' portraits—playing with contrast and unity. My mother's mother made us cotton kimonos with prints that would stick out in any white-bread crowd. My father's sister gave me red, black, and green in pan-African solidarity. When I came to view the world's history, my history, through fabrics, I saw the pain of marginalized groups as rough canvas—shoes and banners of protest, red as love and hate, sequins as revolution. My color philosophy boils down to not playing favorites: I believe that every color is exactly right in some time and capacity, be it the doo-doo brown that is life-giving soil, or the effervescent chartreuse that gives yellow dimension. From an early age, I've despised the 6-color rainbow because of its limitations. My personal style knows no limits—in proportions, color, fabrics, fit. My fashion isn't intended to be a statement, and yet my buttoned-up button down, wide-legged trousers, and sharp cut-away blazer in an iridescent crocodile pattern seems to make one anyway. Maybe you can't pin me down or make it make sense. The fluidity of my clothes pays homage to my ancestors—women who took on "men's" roles and became both parents, working class folks whose uniforms have become androgynous fashion staples. I carry my queer on the soles of my feet and I walk with purpose.

TIG KASHALA is a costume designer, photographer, art history student, and organizer from Southwest Little Rock, Arkansas. Their work has been seen onstage at The Arkansas Repertory Theatre, and at the time of this publication, they are co-organizing Arkansas' first queer and trans people of color assembly. Currently, they are in school at UA Little Rock pursuing an Interdisciplinary Bachelor of Arts degree.

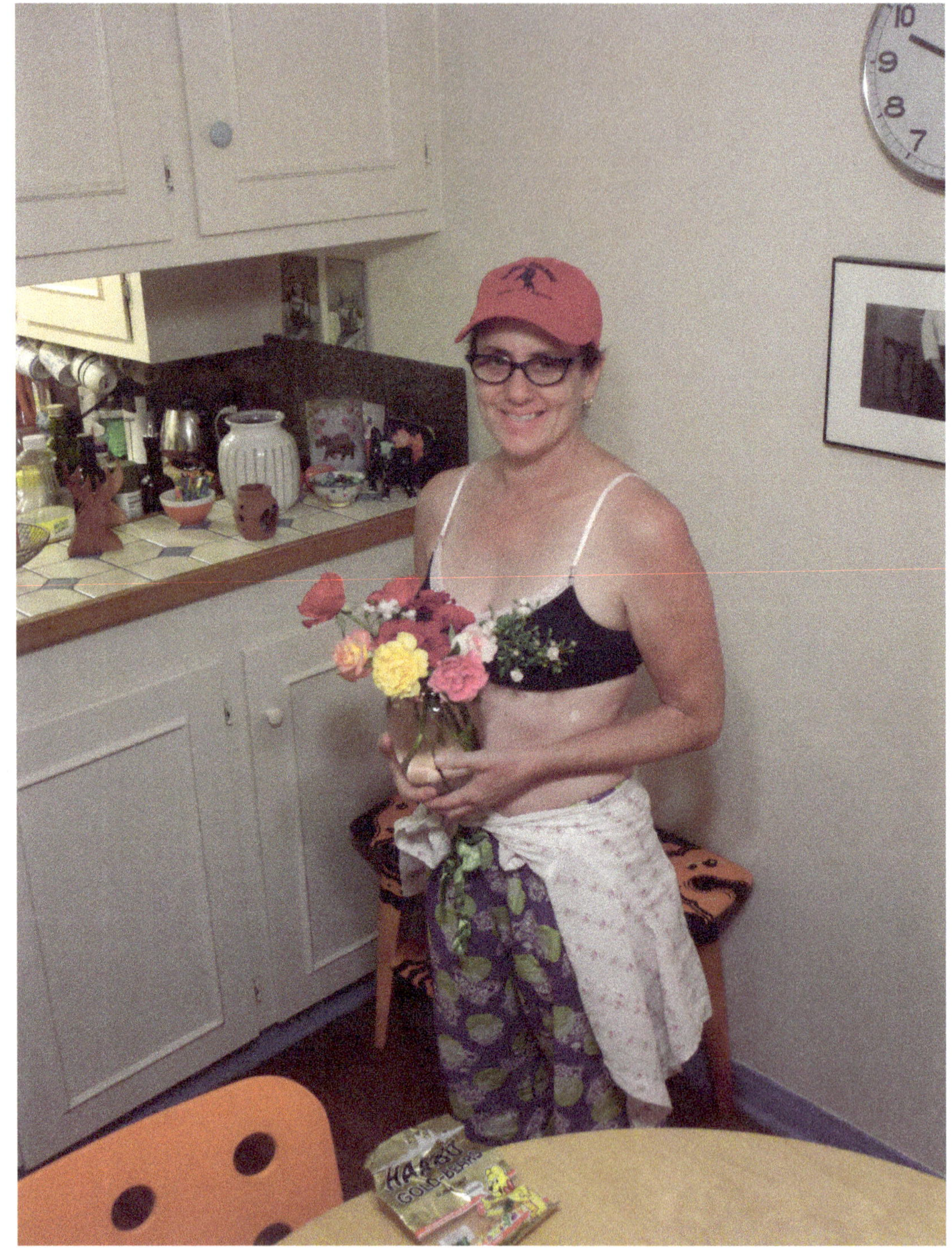

UNREHEARSED

Mostly I'd hide I was muscular
with breasts, layering shirts and
jackets—only at home unrehearsed.

Purple pajama bottoms, royal
rabbits and crowns. Summer
sleep bra from a parking lot
sale near USC. Tomato red
cap you picked for me at Cowgirl
Creamery, souvenir of lesbians
who love dairy. Spray of heirloom
roses from our garden, a jar.
Shirt tied at my waist like a man
might. Dressed in Sunday comfort,
reading glasses, an earring or two.

Now every outfit needs forethought,
prosthetic left breast, still-fresh
scars, a dressing, our new life together.

BONNIE S. KAPLAN is a poet, a native Angeleno, and a longtime teacher of formerly incarcerated adults in reentry. She holds an MFA from California College of the Arts in Film/Video/Performance Art. She is grateful to photographer Sylvia Sukop for this portrait taken in their home in Altadena, California.

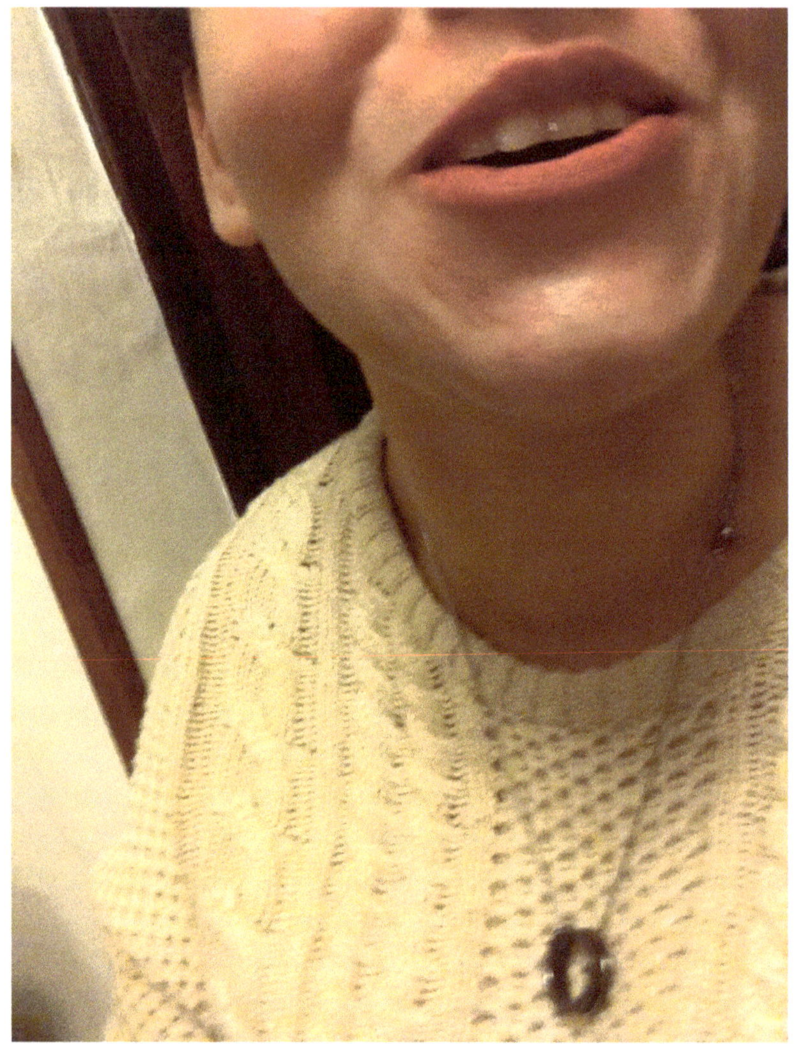

NOUR KAMEL is perfectly lit and writes things from Cairo, Egypt. Kamel is a writer and editor, a *Winter Tangerine* workshop alumnus, and was shortlisted for the Brunel University International African Poetry Prize (2018). Kamel writes about identity, language, sexuality, queerness, gender, oppression, femininity, trauma, family, lineage, globalisation, loss, and food. Their chapbook *Noon* is part of the New-Generation African Poets (Sita) series, and their writing appears in *Asameena*, *Anomaly*, *Rusted Radishes*, and *Khabar Keslan*.

HER SWEATER

was beige and big and for something called a man but she stole bought it dunno it was hers now and it was perfect because it was hers and you took it she let you wear it and you were neither man or her or not but that sweater. That sweater felt so good and you never knew if it was because of her because it was her that envy love wanting to be or or was it the sweater itself made you imagine possibilities you felt knew maybe could impossible then now forever? fear rips between your elbows that have a hard time touching when you wear a bra so why wear a bra in baggy beautiful beige sweater and no one notices or cares what you are in the cold bundled but you don't live in the cold now forever, be careful I love you don't let it get caught on old furniture claws trying to get you your sweater pick a thread loose and loose loose and spooling pooling yourself into possibilities inside clothing your body becomes neglect, a relic you forget because it is more convenient until they make you remember with eyes words lips you'd rather not just let's not and how will you return it to her, her who let you, so much, so many things, let be and all things at once and everything god. But eventually she made, you had, to get your own beige sweater to blend in with yourself the cold it was good, too. You were still beautiful felt whole still, too. On your own, sweater.

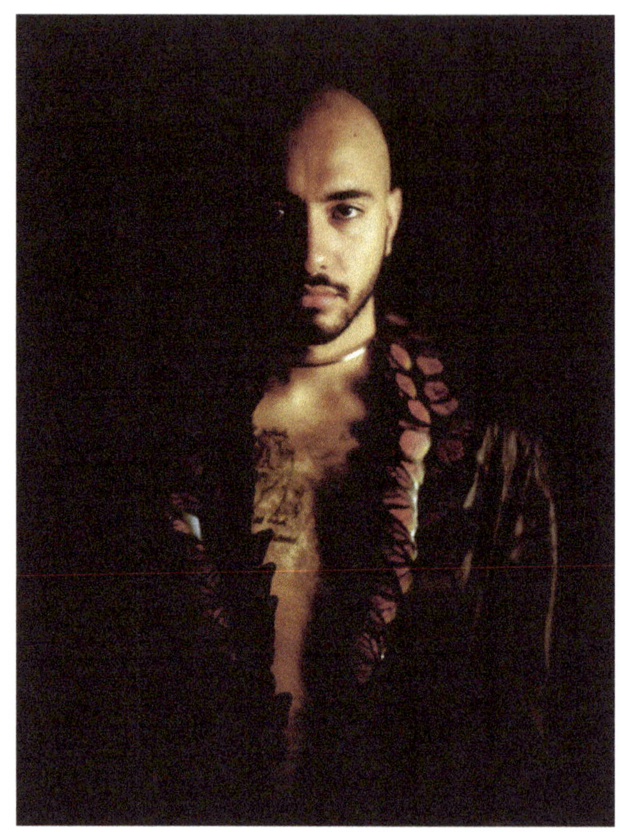

BRANDON KAFARELA is motivated and inspired by an array of vibrant cultures. Brandon is currently based in Houston, in the Urban South where he was born and raised. His personal art encompasses the cultures, languages, colors, relationships, and experiences that have shaped him throughout his life. Brandon uses art to bring all of these elements together to further establish his identity and commitment to his communities. Today, he works as a writer, wardrobe stylist, and costume designer in Texas and Louisiana. Photo by Nick Shamblott.

This genuine-leather jacket was a gift from my grandma. I love when family and friends bring me clothes that actually cater to my taste and aesthetic! (It makes me feel like they truly understand.) I try to collect pieces that are timeless. I never have been someone to shift my style based on new trends—if anything, my style just evolves. This jacket is something I will cherish forever because: 1. It's a thoughtful gift from my grandmother, and 2. It's a versatile garment that can elevate any simple look I put together. The choker is a statement piece from an American Apparel store that was in Houston (R.I.P.). Though American Apparel is considered fast fashion, I do think they upheld the value for simple, well-made pieces, and this choker is a piece that I continuously wear, years after its purchase. The butterflies I used to ornament the lapel of this jacket were gifted to me by a Mexico City-based photographer and dear friend, David Romero @lordmariposa. The butterflies were a recurring theme during my time in Mexico. David adopted me into his family of mariposas, and as butterflies travel and migrate, so do we. I love these butterflies. They've connected me to so many dear friends, experiences, and opportunities. They're a symbol and reminder of the way I want to exist and the types of people I want to connect with as I grow. The outfit featured in this photo is a solid representation of how I love to use my body as a canvas and clothes as my medium of choice to express myself, my culture, and art.

Fashion was always a safe haven for me while growing up in environments and communities where my identity may not have always been welcome. As someone who wasn't too vulnerable to the outside world through words, fashion led me to the people and places where I could truly be myself. I am thrilled to say that fashion and wardrobe has now become a principal medium for my art and professional career. My mission is to use fashion to uplift our communities alongside like-minded artists and professionals with a shared commitment to create purposeful visual and written works of art.

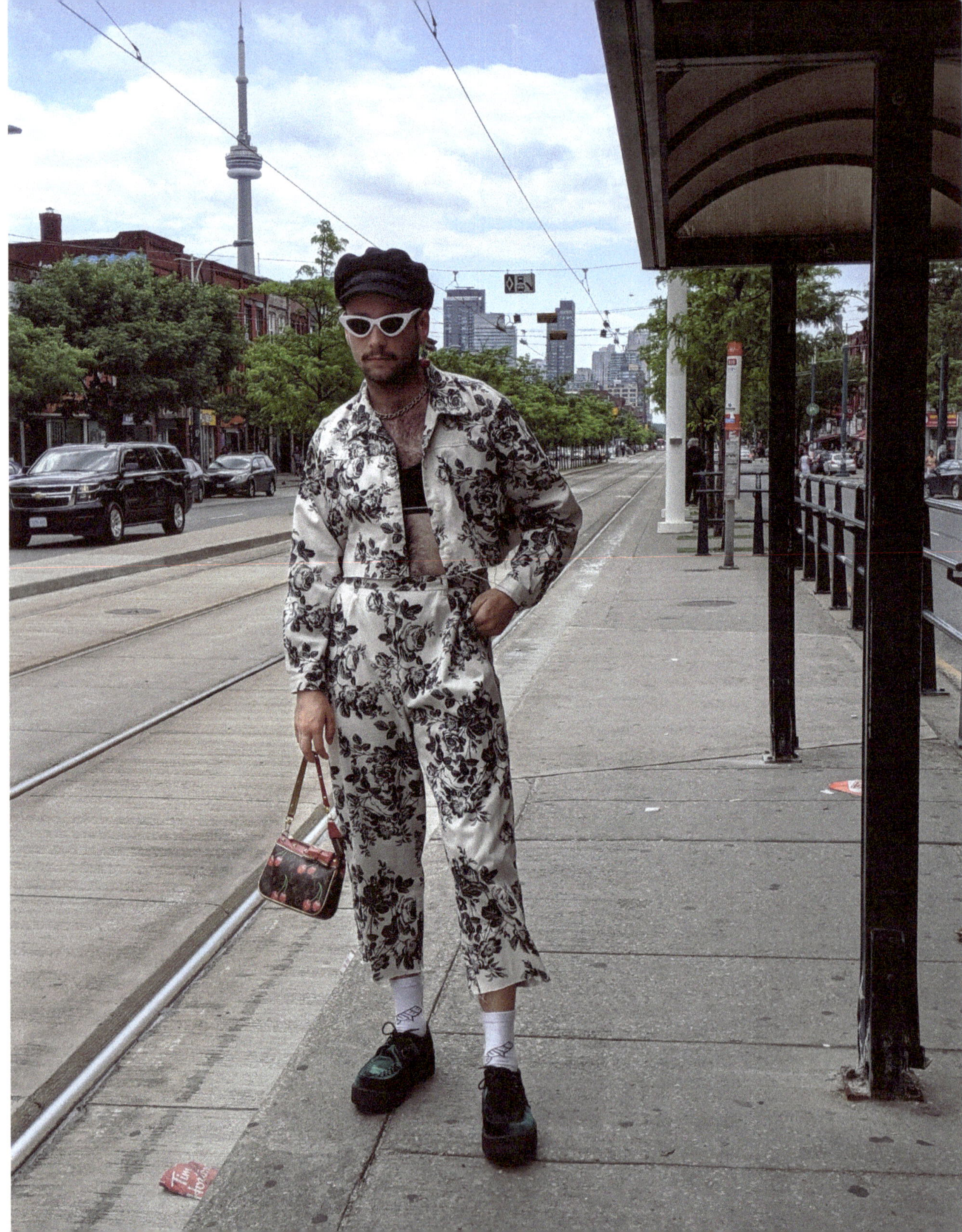

THRIFT NANNY LOOK

This floral thrifted look is the inspiration behind "thrift nanny." This look represents a pivotal point in my gender expression and style journey. Style and fashion are so closely related to my journey to self-acceptance. Clothes allow me to be seen as the person I've always felt I am on the inside.

One day I was thrifting, feeling slightly nervous while browsing the "women's" section for anything I could turn a look in. I found this beautiful floral set and saw so much potential, but not yet perfection. It looked exactly the way it was supposed to, like your nan's fave two-piece blouse set. I rushed home and got straight to work with some sheers and voilà! Thrift Nanny was born.

Thrifting has been routine for me ever since I've been buying my own clothes. I learned about the environmental and humanitarian epidemic that is the garment industry, and realized that the systems that are neglecting our planet and the garment workers are the same systems that are harming queer folx. From then on, I've thrifted most of my clothes, and when I don't, I do my best to make informed purchases.

This traditionally "women's" outfit was one of the first outfits that made me feel affirmed in my femme body. It shows off the right amount of femme, fun, hairy playfulness that I've grown to love in myself. It's an indirect, non-verbal, non-exhausting way of saying that I'm over the gender binary and its restrictions. I've spent so much time trying to conform and fit into a standard of beauty that was created by people who aim to silence people like me. Clothing has set me free from that; it is the constant in all of this that brings me joy, playfulness, and a sense of self.

Style and fashion, to me, mean that I get to shout from the roof tops (or these velvet green platforms) that I've given up on carrying the weight of my own and everyone else's internalized transphobia and hatred for non-conformity. It is no longer my problem, and I look SO much better without that weight on my shoulders, don't I?

KAI JACKMAN is a non-binary trans femme model, aspiring stylist, and fashion influencer from the Greater Toronto Area who strives to queerify the sustainable fashion scene while looking fine as hell.

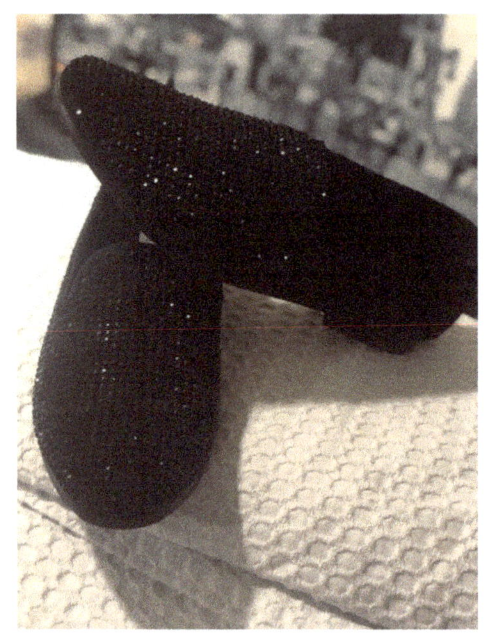

CLEO HOUSE, JR., is Director of the School of Theatre at Stephen F. Austin State University. House is a director, writer, actor, and teacher.

LITTLE BLACK TEXAS BOY AND THE GLITTERY SHOES

A little black Texas boy, sitting in the shade
He ain't got no toy, so he plays with something
        homemade.

Looks like momma has gone, he bounces to the
        trailer and turns MTV on.

Sashay shuntay walking down the hallway

The little black Texas boy, in his momma's heels
Switching and twitching, booty moving like it was
        itchin'

The heels were black and made him feel tall
In that shiny shellac, he owned it all

Emotional brakes screeching, little brother is
        home
Snatching off the towel wig from his big brother's
        dome

Outside little brother goes, straight to uncle under
        the car connecting a hose.

The little black Texas boy froze in disgrace
Uncle approaches him with a question mark on
        his face.

"You know we ain't got no sissies around here
        in these parts? You wanna break your
        momma's heart?"

Tears in his eyes, and this is no exaggeration.
The little black boy learned to avoid true expression.

Years passed and the little black boy is all grown
        up with a tendency to please
He's a masculine black gay man cause "ain't no
        sissies" was a lesson he learned with ease.

Three days before the party and still nothing to
        wear
To the mall he goes, the last trip he swears

He spies a pair of glittery pumps but walks away,
        "Who do I think I am—Beyonce?"
He returns to the rack, "Do you have these in a
        size 13 in the back?"

Slipping on the glittery black shoes...he is
        transported

Serving glamour
        Sashay shantay walking down the runway
Serving attitude
        Werk, werk, werk, werk, werk
Serving sophistication
        Call me mother!

The glittery black shoes were the first step giving
        myself permission to be seen and take up
        space.

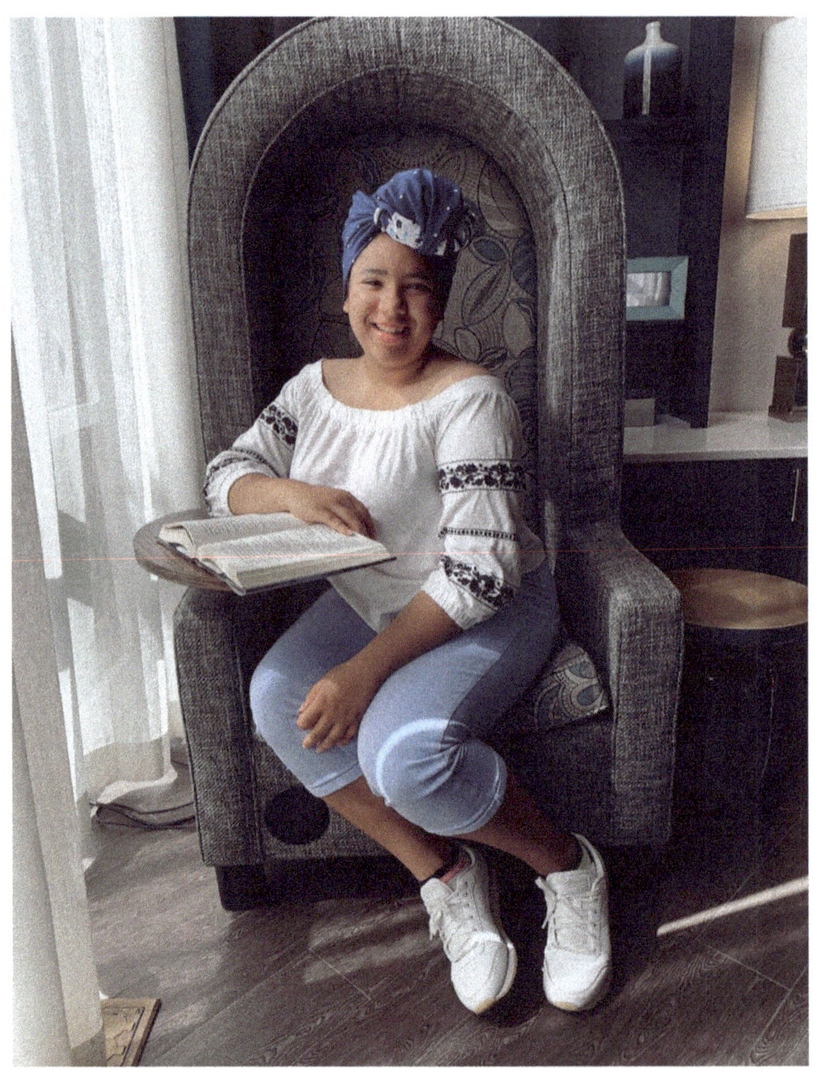

SARAH HOLSTON is a student who is currently exploring many passions. In all spheres that she participates in, her identity as a member of the QTPOC community allows her to gain unique perspectives and feel pride at being her authentic self.

CHILD OF ALL

He told her, "This will protect you."
Larger hands embraced smaller and a scarf fluttered between two generations.
How could silk take up shield and sword in the streets of Kampala?
And her image: the girl who is the daughter of a fighter,
the woman who defines normal and settles for extraordinary.
One might say they are one and the same.
But she cares for that scarf more than we know.
And while it rests atop her head, centuries of traditions and
Culture balanced on a strong neck, her mind flutters
With the joys and breaths of the future.

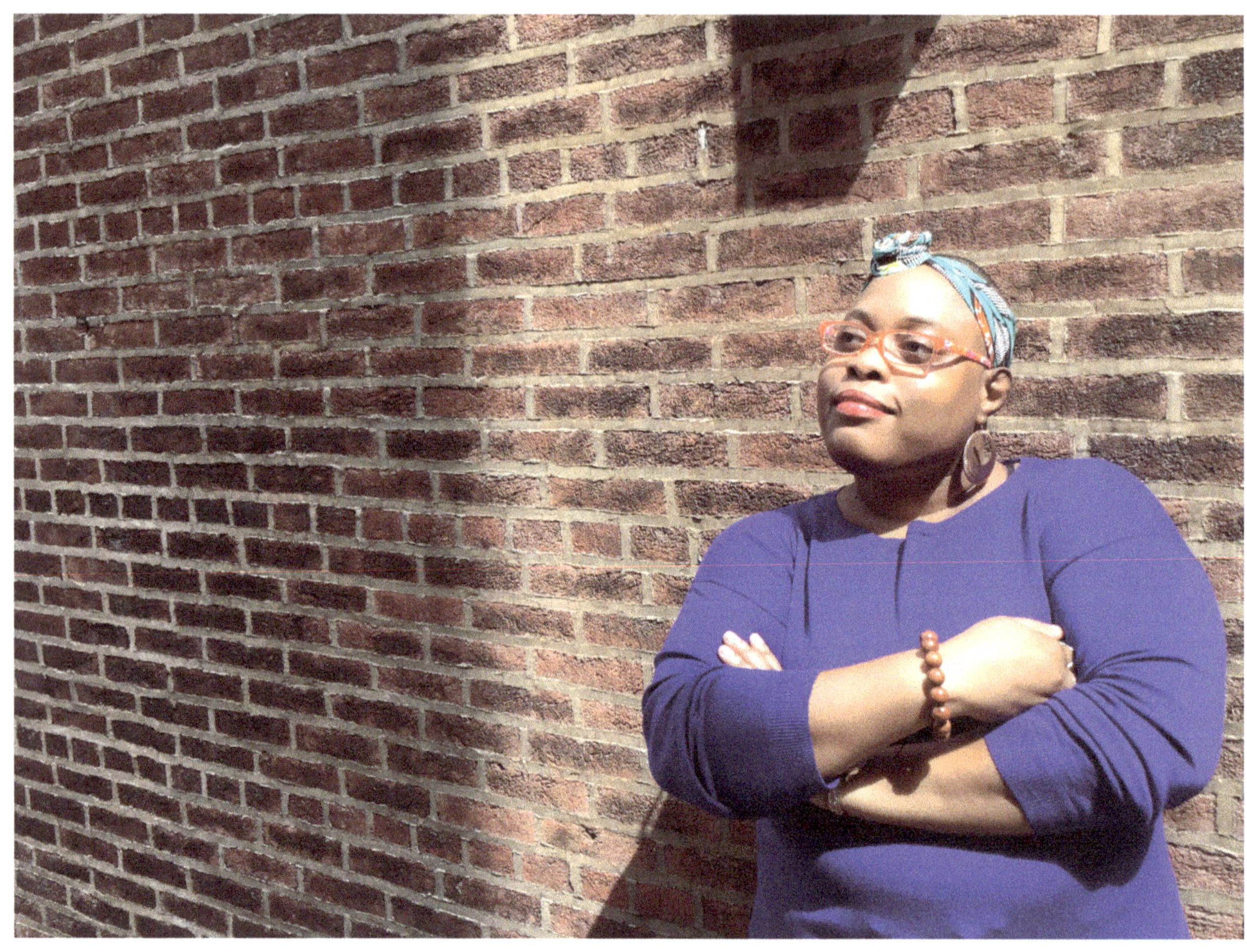

TS HAWKINS is an international author, performance poet, artivist, and emerging playwright. Plays and short works include: *Seeking Silence, Cartons of Ultrasounds, Too Late to Apologize, They'll Neglect to Tell You, #RM2B, The Secret Life of Wonder: A Prologue in G, AGAIN, #SuiteReality*, and *don't wanna dance with ghosts* . . . Hawkins' one-act choreopoem, *AGAIN*, was acknowledged for having the "Best Theater Moment of 2017" along with *#SuiteReality* receiving a Surya Bonaly Award and publication in *WORDPEACE Literary Journal*. Books include: *Sugar Lumps & Black Eye Blues; Confectionately, Yours; Mahogany Nectar; Lil Black Book: all the long stories short;* and *The Hotel Haikus*. Hawkins is most known for the Poetry Master Class, "Thriving Ain't Easy," a course that infuses health, wellness, and activism through poetry.

ADORNMENT

masked in conservative solids
hiding ingenuity in folded uncertainty
the abstract concept no one could fashion
fell upon deaf ears and silenced accents
doleful;
a fragmented accessory
laying costumed
acid washed
sutured in black and blue revelations dying slow
perishing in baubled sound bytes
respirated only by the remnants;
the opposed pattern pushing at seams
rimmed lenses dusted in tangerine refrains
rose colored watches move time
to swatch fine printed faux pas
head wrapped in the hash-marks
azure hued in past headlines
twirling a slated reality of the you they never knew
the undisclosed closure of the masses
a curved leatherette sketch
pounded and ground into unclaimed vintage
discounted
mined to obscurity

you wear a mask
to protect brown frames from anti-black silhouettes
sacred memories dangling
by liberty seeking lobes
screaming not to be long forgotten
in the fabric of a nation strutting erasure
the spruce reminder of commercial algorithms
sharing a part of you
they never cared to mend
selvedging hope in sample cloths
you wear a mask
...hopefully,
for not too long

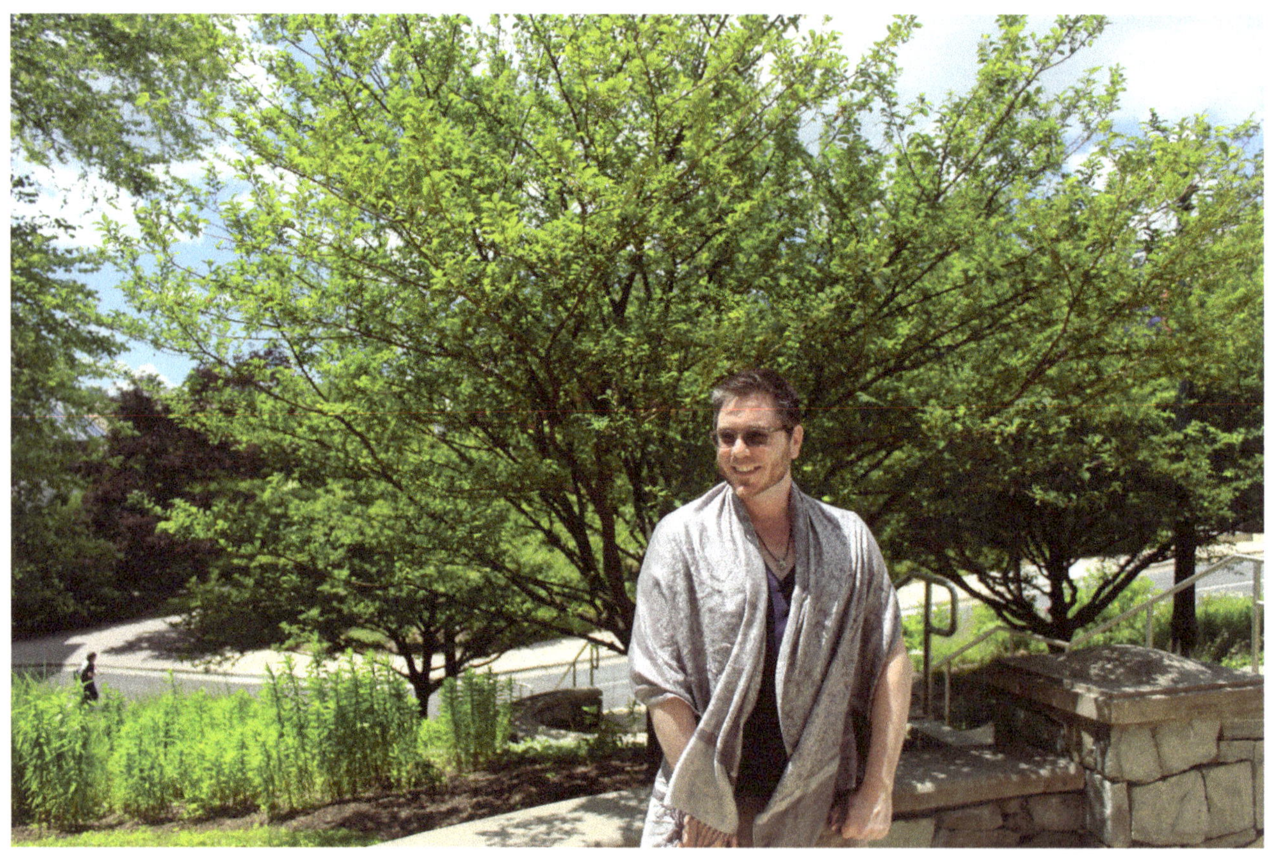

JONATHAN HARPER is the author of the short story collection *Daydreamers* (Lethe Press, 2015), a *Kirkus Review* Indie Book of the Year. He lives in Northern Virginia.

I flew out to visit my grandmother this past winter and made sure I dressed in the way my parents would approve: a dress shirt and slacks and a fitted blazer. The scarf was my favorite. Long gray linen with purple and pink designs folded into the fabric, curved around my neck so the frilly ends dangled as I moved. I would like to think it was the kind of scarf that would make Stevie Nicks jealous.

"I love it," she said and rubbed her fingers over the edge of the fabric. Her smile was coy, the kind grandmothers use when they are guarding a wonderful secret.

I own a lot of scarves, oversized ones I can drape around me like a shawl. I would let them drift out from under my coat or blazer as a small flash of color or fold them neatly across my neck and shoulders like a shield. I pull them up over my mouth when I am caught off guard. I wore these scarves like a barrier. Something to hide behind. To hide or to be seen—that old homo conundrum.

I wondered how many visits I had left with my grandmother, how many more times I had to speak with her in private. She was ninety-four; I was thirty-eight. It was already time to leave. It had been a pleasant visit.

"I have something for you," she said. She moved methodically, rummaging through the little chest in her room at the assisted living facility, and retrieved one of her own scarves, one I'd seen her wear before. It was silver with an abstract floral print, an elegant, matronly scarf that shimmered when the light hit it. "I want you to have this," she said. "You can wear it if you like."

And I did.

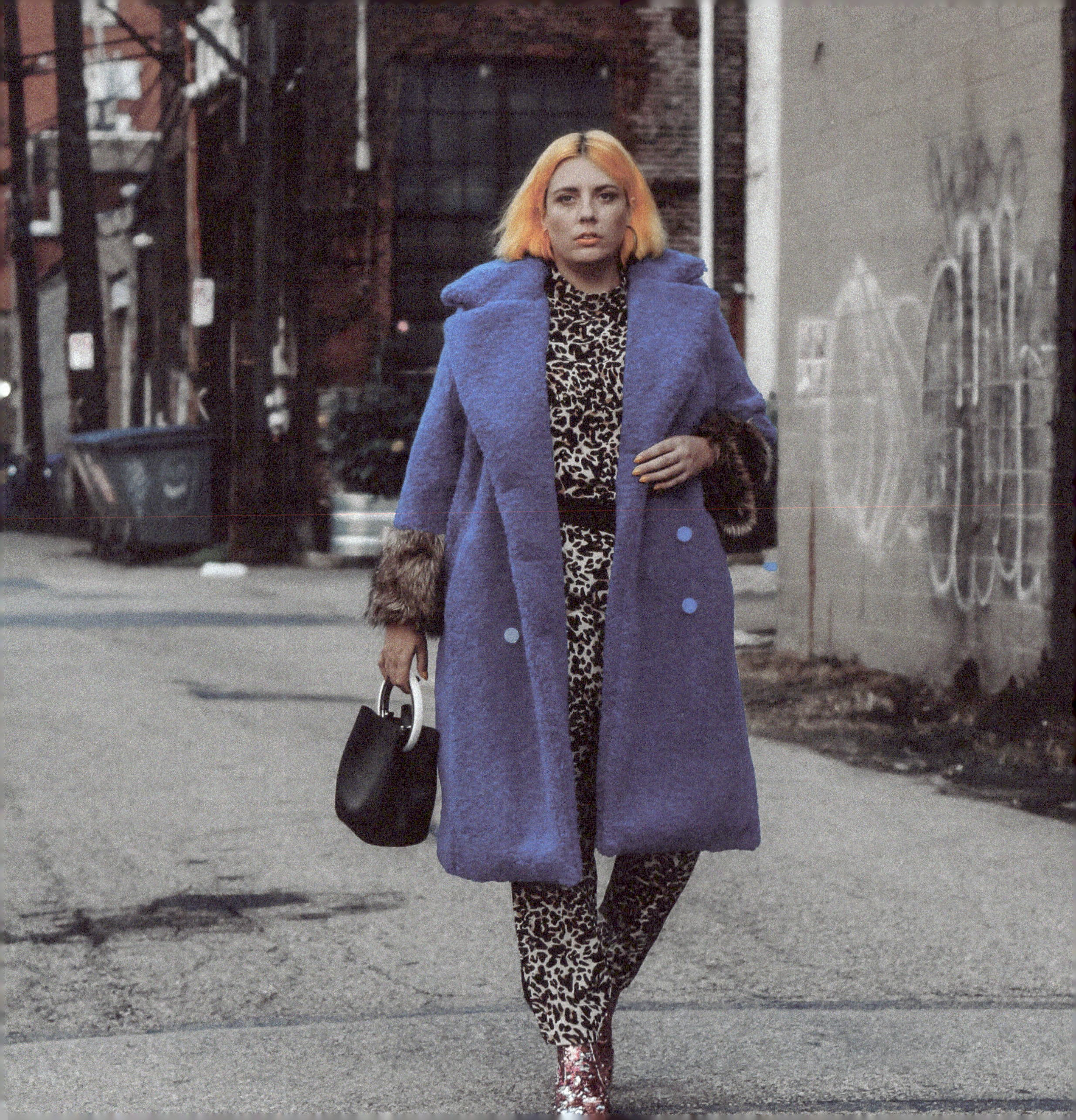

This look is essential Jamie. Statement making, comfortable, and a nod to vintage. I dress to take up visual space and to attract other weirdos in my life. As a fat and tall person, there is a societal pressure to blend into the background. I embrace my aesthetic: tacky regal and a bit ugly. Pink sequin boots, bright blue teddy jacket with faux fur trim over an animal print set in contrast to my near makeup-less face except for a swipe of lipstick and messy, dyed hair.

A friend pointed out to me that David Bowie wore a similar coat in the 1970s. And I wasn't surprised as Bowie has been my style inspiration since I first studied my parents' Bowie record covers at age eleven. A lot of 70s glam with a dose of space alien.

Queer visionary and artist GB Jones drew a picture of teenage Jamie. I was eighteen. I remember what I was wearing: blue combat boots, blue vinyl jacket, and dyed orange hair. The pencil drawing, however, was devoid of color in classic Jones style. The illustration was published in a book where the author described me as the super girl next door, which was pretty cool, but I'd like to think I've evolved into an electrifying fat femme from outer space.

JAMIE HAMILTON is a plus size style creative director known as Jamie JeTaime. She was featured in *InStyle Magazine* for her street style and named by MTV UK as an influencer to look out for in 2019. She regularly hosts body positive swim parties and currently lives in Tucson, Arizona.

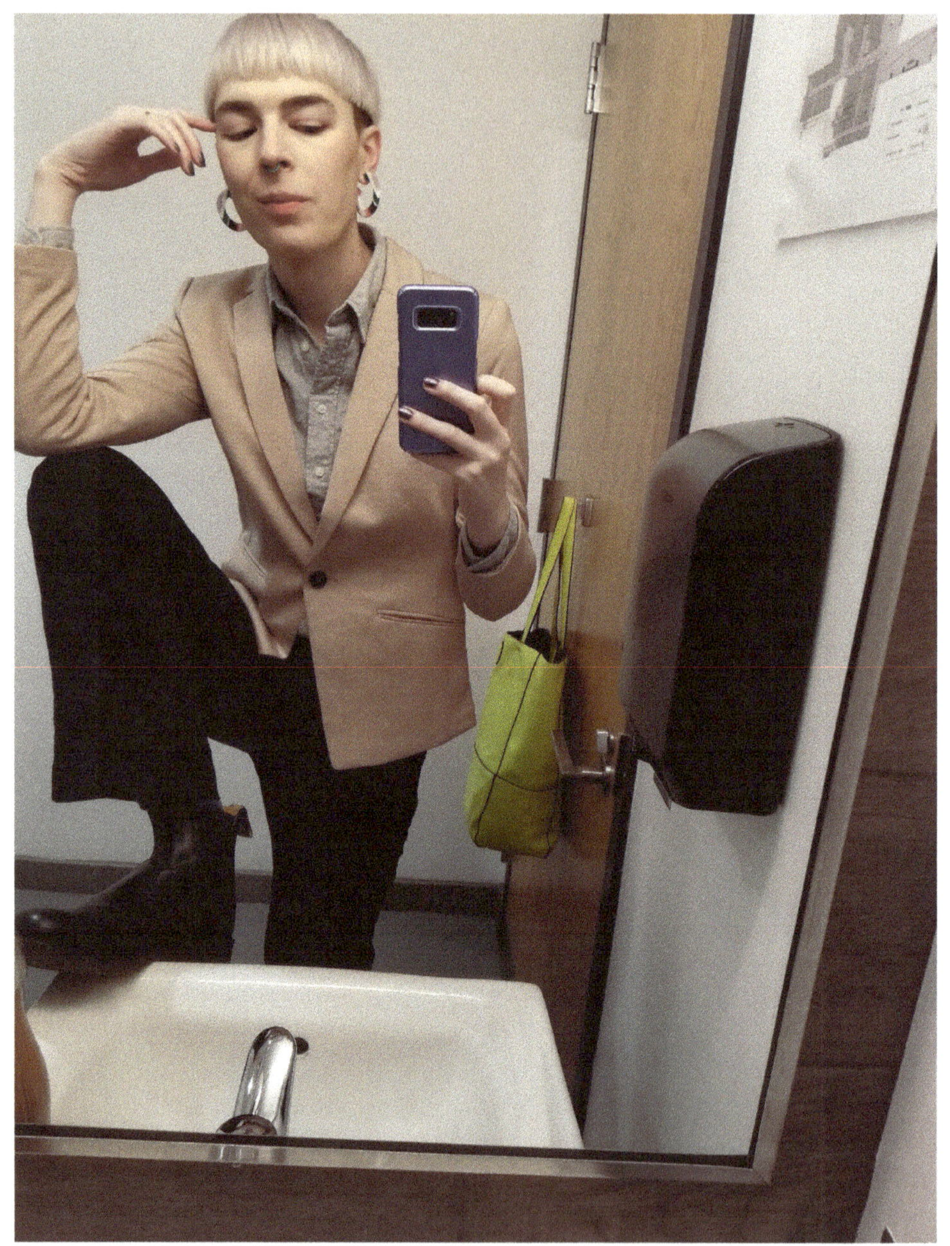

BERRY GRASS is the author of *Hall of Waters* (The Operating System, 2019). Their essays appear in *DIAGRAM*, *The Normal School*, *Barrelhouse*, and *Territory*, among other publications. They were a 2019 nominee for the Krause Essay Prize.

#BLAZERFEMME

In 1947, Christian Dior showed his first haute couture collection in Paris. The hallmark of the collection, which fashion critics would hail as "the New Look," was what he called the Bar Jacket: a blazer for women (a novel concept in the 1940s) with long darting, wide shoulders, and a blown out peplum bottom. An exaggeratedly feminine shape achieved with a garment usually reserved for men's business or sporting pursuits.

I think this was the second blazer I ever bought. H&M, not Dior of course. It's a sort of blushy salmon color with an off-white lining. A single button, walnut brown. I can dress it up for teaching with black pinstripe trousers, or I can dress it down with jeans or a sweater or a tee. Does the darted waist and the soft pink help me be seen as the woman I am? If I'm read as a man does it give off a prissy, dandy queer Oscar Wilde/Walter Pater Victorian aesthete vibe? Does it carry both answers at once, like I want it to, a marker of gender nonconformity from any angle?

Some know me around my city by the social media hashtag I use for selfies, #BlazerFemme. If I had to describe my weird gender in a single phrase, I think Blazer Femme would do the trick. I feel most feminine, most womanly, and most desirable when I'm wearing suits, blazers, button down collared shirts, trousers, boots—"menswear." Winged eyeliner and dangly earrings and a sharp beam of highlighter to signify my femmeness, yes, but it's like my body doesn't believe in itself without feeling fabric frame my ribcage, without the jacket's soft drape over my shoulders.

Darting is a folding and tucking and sewing of flat fabric to create shape. Darts make room for your bust, or accentuate the curve of your midsection. An alteration so that you look how you want to look. When the darted waist of a tailored blazer wraps around me, I feel gently held. My trans body, which I have altered so that I look how I want to look, recognizes itself in the embrace.

When everyone thought I was a boy, I hid my body in oversized clothes and shoes two sizes too big. The black suit jacket I had for funerals was large, shapeless, something I could be invisible in. And all the while, the people whose style and whose bodies I saw some of myself in were those of queer women. Since transitioning, I've started to wear things like workwear overalls, ribbed tank tops, and sneakers. Clothes that felt like a prison sentence because of my queerness now feel liberating on my body because of my queerness.

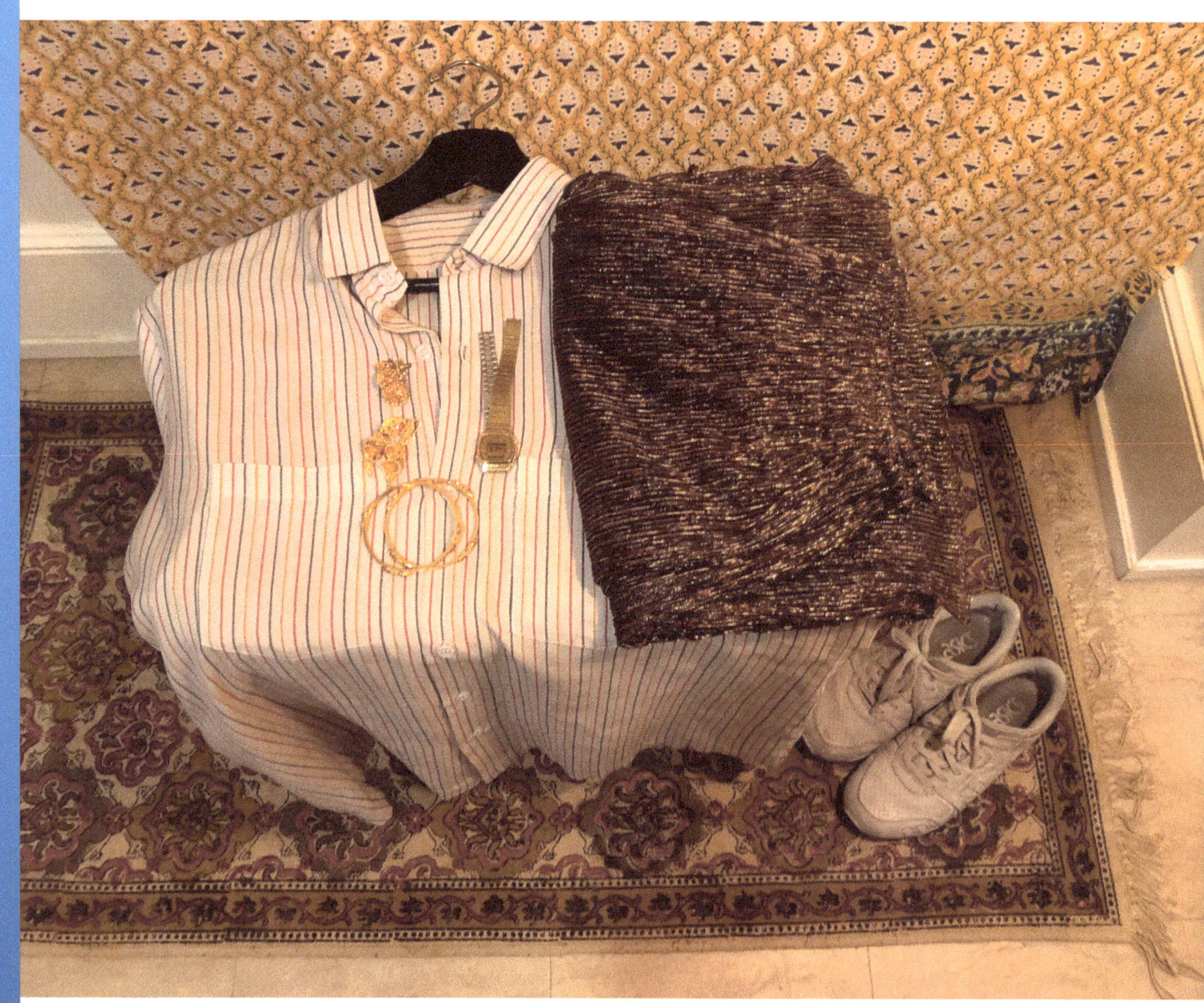

WEARING DOUBLE JHUMKAS, GIFTED BANGLES, AND THE GOLD CASIO MY OLDEST FRIEND ALSO HAS

So many of the things I wear every day have personal histories spindling out behind them: I wear my dad's pants, my mom's scarves, my brother's shoes, my grandmother's jewelry, my friend's shirts, another friend's grandma's sweaters. This isn't quite my way of holding my loved ones close (although I suppose it does do that)—my daily wear is an unintentional accumulation, not a curated effort. My clothes are outward-facing manifestations of many little interactions, all their looped lineages tangling invisibly when I put them on.

My mother once told me she doesn't have a country anymore. We were standing in her closet, surrounded by American and Indian clothes collected over a lifetime, which seems appropriately poignant, and this instability came as a surprise. (My parents, in my mind, are infinite possessors of a stability that opposes my instability.)

Every time Ma reteaches me how to drape a sari before a function, because I know how to do it in theory but it's been too long since last time, she tells me about the textile tradition and regional history it's a part of. She tells me how long she likes the fall of the pallu over her shoulder, and that my Dida, her mother, can make neater, faster pleats. Her sari drawers are thick and full and opened rarely, and there are layers and layers of folded fabric, silk and cotton and embroidery and kalamkari and kantha and kanjivaram and pattu, and some are gifts from Dida and neighborhood aunties from Hyderabad, and some are from shopping trips with ladies from the family. Every time we wade through them together, I listen to these stories and get distracted by everything else in her closet, and by the time we've moved to my room to put the sari on me, I've procured a few shirts and kurtis to "borrow for just one semester."

My closet is an agglomeration that is not comprehensive—an uneven representation of the things these histories signify. I don't run through these stories when I put my clothes on, or link back and back the owners and their stories, but my wearing serves as a carrying, a quiet retelling. Putting on a favorite work shirt of my grandfather's, whom I never met, over shiny pants my closest friend encouraged into my closet, over shoes that grew too small for my brother when we finally stopped sharing a shoe size, feels important and, at the same time, entirely mundane, all this imbricated meaning illegible to people who see me, and to me too, mostly. Wearing, then, becomes a physical comprehension, acknowledgement, layering, of things too tangled to ever properly parse.

AHANA GANGULY is studying English at Pomona College, and she is interested in essayism, diasporic writing, and all kinds of creative nonfiction.

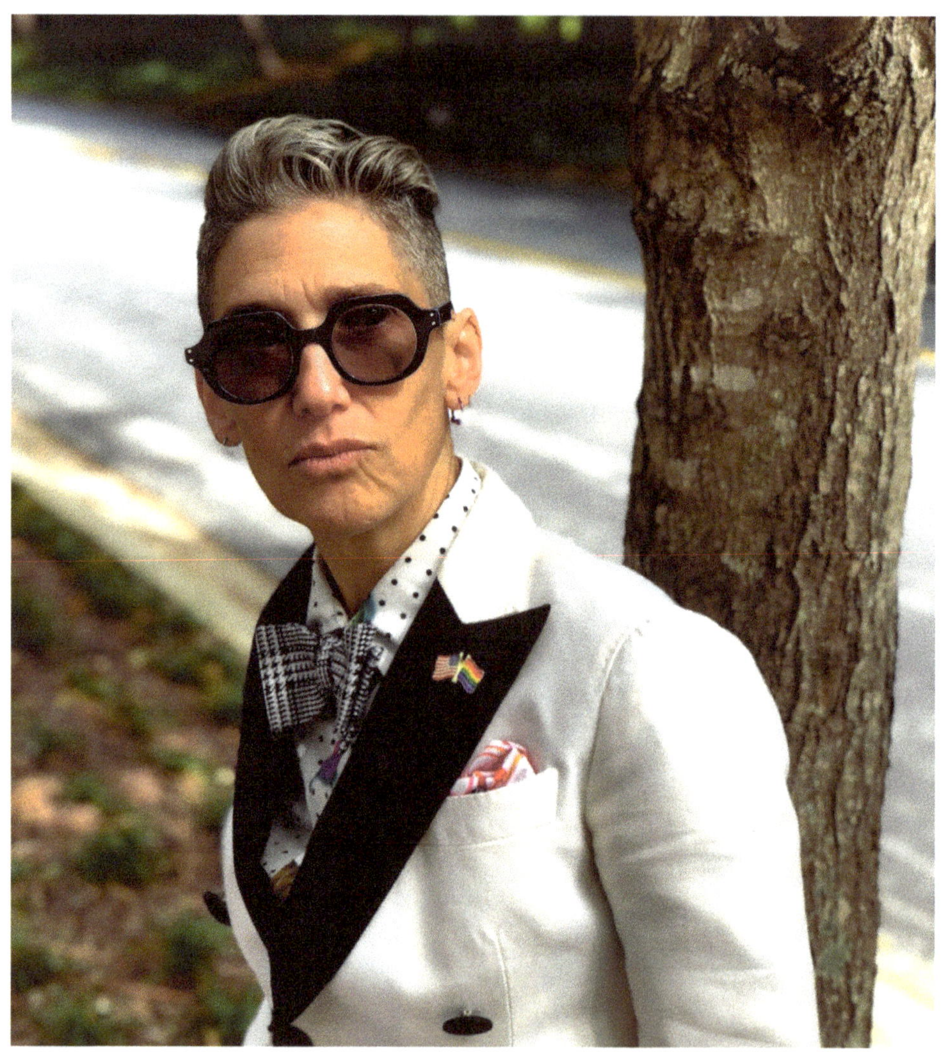

MINDY DAWN FRIEDMAN is a gender non-conforming visual activist, proud auntie to those in need, and the founder of #BowTieWednesday at her place of work. Her bold fashion transgressions have graced the runway at New York Fashion Week and appeared in a handful of national ad campaigns.

THE ART OF THE BOW TIE

I used to wear pre-tied bow ties. I admit it. They are easy and flawless every time. When friends started commenting on my impeccable knotting, I had to either admit the truth or divert the conversation. Authenticity demanded I learn how to 'master' the self-tie bow tie.

Bow ties are the cape, the shield, the removed-Clark-Kent-glasses of my visual activism superhero identity. They carry an air of intellectualism, formality, nerdiness, and style acumen. Wearing a bow tie can be perceived as an aggressive lack of concern for what other people think. A *woman* in a bow tie subverts the gender paradigms of fashion even further. I remember the awe I felt the first time I saw an image of Marlene Dietrich in a bow tie and top hat. The quote below the photo read, "I dress for myself. Not for the image, not for the public, not for the fashion, not for men."

I am no Marlene Dietrich. While I dress for myself first and foremost, I *do* dress for the image, the public, and *to be visible*. My bow ties offer a symbolic optimism that frequently provoke dialogue and connections with others—driving visibility, awareness, and social change.

After significant practice and frustration, I've achieved mastery of the art. No need for a mirror. I take pride in teaching and inspiring others. Personally, I prefer an imperfect knot, mostly as evidence that it was self-tied. It also tends to engage an occasional observer to kindly point out the imperfection, and when appropriate, offer to adjust it.

It's not about being brave. It's about being myself. It is about breaking arbitrary rules to make it easier for those who come after—so that they can fully realize their own identity, voice, and style.

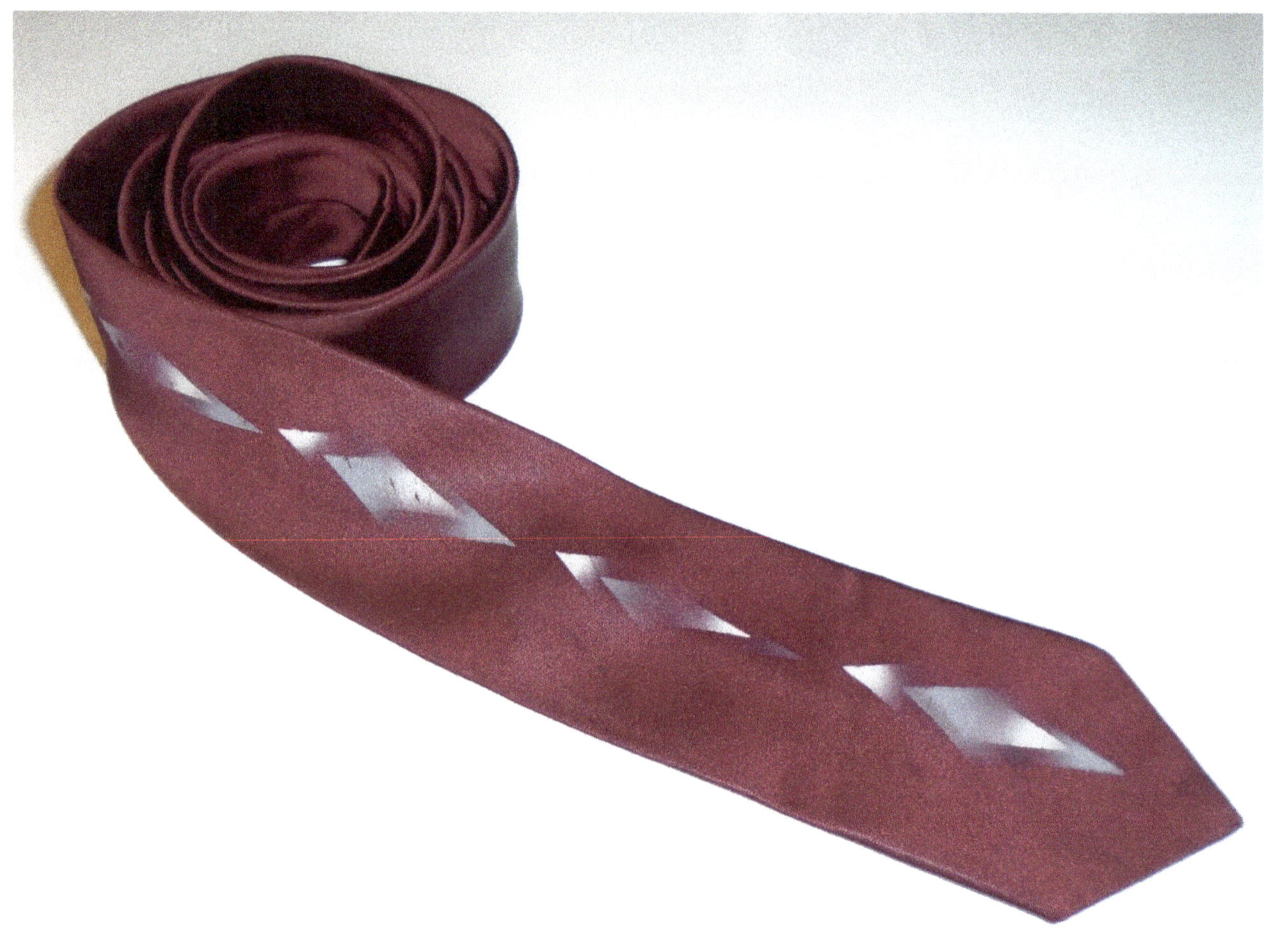

JOY MICHAEL ELLISON is a writer, historian, and organizer. They are interested in using stories and poetry to build community, document social movements, and imagine a liberated world. Their writing has appeared in the *Baltimore Review*, *Lunch Ticket*, *Columbus Alive*, and many other places. They believe that art is integral to healing, transformation, resistance, and survival.

GRANDPA'S TIE

When my grandpa passed away, I wasn't there. My mom said in his final moments, Grandpa asked for me and she lied. She said my goodbye for me. My mom told me this story without looking at me, in a voice so quiet and low that I am not sure that I heard her correctly. She never made me feel guilty. She acted as though she was the one who should be embarrassed.

I missed my grandpa's death because I was nineteen years old, queer, and foolhardy. I had come out to my parents a few months earlier and Mom had detailed the ways my sexuality was hard on her. Unable to shoulder the burden of her feelings, I ran away.

When Mom emailed me to say Grandpa was dying, I thought it was a ploy to lure me home. Reality gripped me in the middle of the night. I rushed to a payphone. I was the only one surprised when Mom told me that Grandpa had already died.

I will never know why Mom gave me Grandpa's necktie after his funeral. There may have been no reason, as she gave me his flannel pajamas, too. Or maybe she realized, with some maternal sixth sense, that I would wear ties more than my Grandpa ever did.

When I was little, Grandpa would lift me into the seat of his blue Ford pick-up and fasten the seat belt. He always slid on a metal clip that held the strap down low, so that it ran across the chest of my small body instead of cutting into my neck. He bought me department store jewelry, heart-shaped necklaces and bracelets with my name and birthstone. The shine of it appealed to me, but I never wore it. I do, however, wear his tie.

If my Grandpa had lived longer, I might have disappointed him. I was his oldest grandchild and he treated me like his two daughters. He was comfortable around girls. I'm not sure he would approve of my queer, non-binary swagger and swish, but I don't care. I'm still giving him the opportunity to love me. I'm still saying my goodbyes.

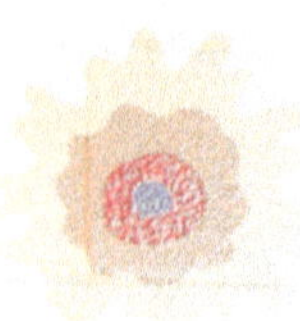
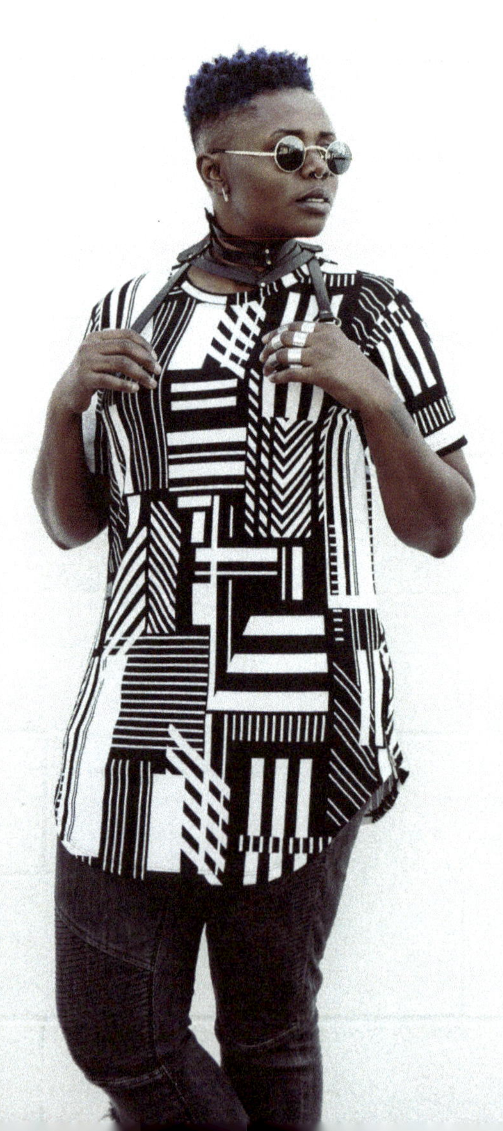

As a noun, fashion is defined as a popular trend and as a verb its synonyms are construct, create, fabricate, make, and build. No matter the definition, the LGBTQ+ community has continued to use fashion as a way of self-expression, PRIDE, and resistance against hate. As a community that has been told that who we are doesn't fit the "normal" society in which we live or that we are less than because of our sexuality, we've found ways to live unapologetically through fashion.

I was born in Nigeria, where I remember mostly wearing dresses and skirts growing up. I don't remember being told I couldn't wear pants, but I had the understanding that women didn't wear pants. As I got older and lived in Spain with my aunt, I remember a specific outfit that I chose for myself, which consisted of a pair of baggy pants and a cropped tank top. I remember being so happy. I felt like my true self.

As I get older, I have found a balance between expressing my masculinity and femininity through fashion. Some days I like to wear dresses and some days I like to wear more masculine presenting, affirming clothing. I am discovering that I like leather, which I like to add as accessories. I also love wearing prints that speak to my African background. It all depends on how I feel that day. Whatever I'm feeling on the inside is how I like to present on the outside. In this image I wanted to show my hard femme vibes with a leather choker and a leather harness while wearing an extended long print t-shirt with some jeans. Those details I feel elevate my look.

The queer community thrives on authenticity; therefore, it is equally important for us to use fashion to express our identity, which we hold so dear. As time passes, it's become increasingly inspiring to see the evolution of the queer community's stamp and influence on the fashion world. I see mainstream brands adapting to what the queer community is doing and creating, to follow the trend. What makes us light up as individuals is our desire to be seen as our true selves and we are able to communicate that through fashion. We are not interested in fitting in, especially not in a world that decided to label us as outsiders. The more expressive an outfit is, the better! The bolder an outfit is, the better! The more colorful an outfit is, the better!

"The category is . . . LIVE!!!"

UZO EJIKEME was born in Nigeria, lived in Spain for 4 years, then in New York for over 15 years before moving to Los Angeles, where she currently lives. One of her fondest memories growing up was her first haircut; that was the first time she felt like her true self represented in physical form.

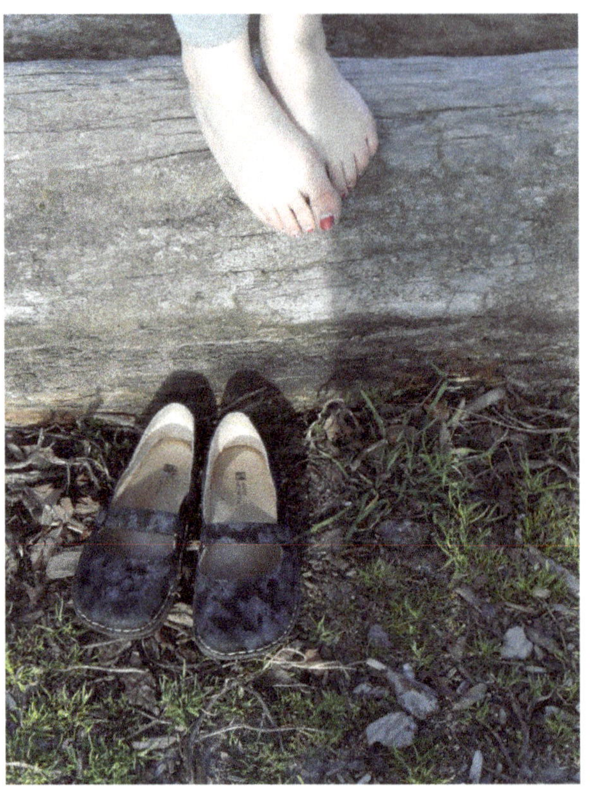

ANGIE EBBA is a queer disabled femme. As a writer, educator, activist, and performance artist, she believes strongly in the transformative powers of words and performance. She teaches and performs across the United States. Angie is a published essayist and poet, as well as teaching online and in-person writing workshops. She fully believes in the power of words to help us gain a better understanding of ourselves, to build connections and community, and to make personal and social change.

HEELS

I.
Click-clack click-clack click-clack click-clack
I mean business
Long steps as I stride across college hallways
Off to make the world right
If only for one student
          Patent leather pumps

Thunder crash of a room full of hands against
hands
Yelling from fans
My face glowing as I stand
Clothes scattered across stage
Arms above head
Pasties, thong, and nothing else but my
          Black bowed burlesque heels

Silent stare as I stand in crowded courtroom
Damn you
Damn you
Don't you dare mess with my
Babies
          Kiss ass and take names stilettos

Laughing
Eyes locked
Skin kissed salty with sweat
Drunk boys spilling beer on my feet
I don't care baby, I don't care
I just want you, I just want you, just
          Take me home and fuck me heels

II.
White kitchen trash bag
Mouth open
Swallowing pair after pair after pair

As I throw them in, while
I sit on the floor in pain
Angry at my body
Grieving
So much wrapped up in that leather, satin, glitter
So much of who I am
So many memories in those soles
Crying in my
          Slippers

III.
My children screaming
Chasing each other around the yard
I smile and breathe in the grass
          Denim blue high tops

Clapping and hollering
My voice hoarse from screaming
My glitter community on stage performing for me
Loving me by dancing when I can't
I sit surrounded by friends
          Red velvet Mary Janes

Florence and the Machine floating into
The kitchen as my love cooks
Grabbing me around the waist
Cheek to cheek
Rocking in a slow dance
          Barefoot

Words tumbling one upon another
In dark-paneled room
Eyes watching my eyes fill with tears
Letting go and accepting
          Black strappy flats

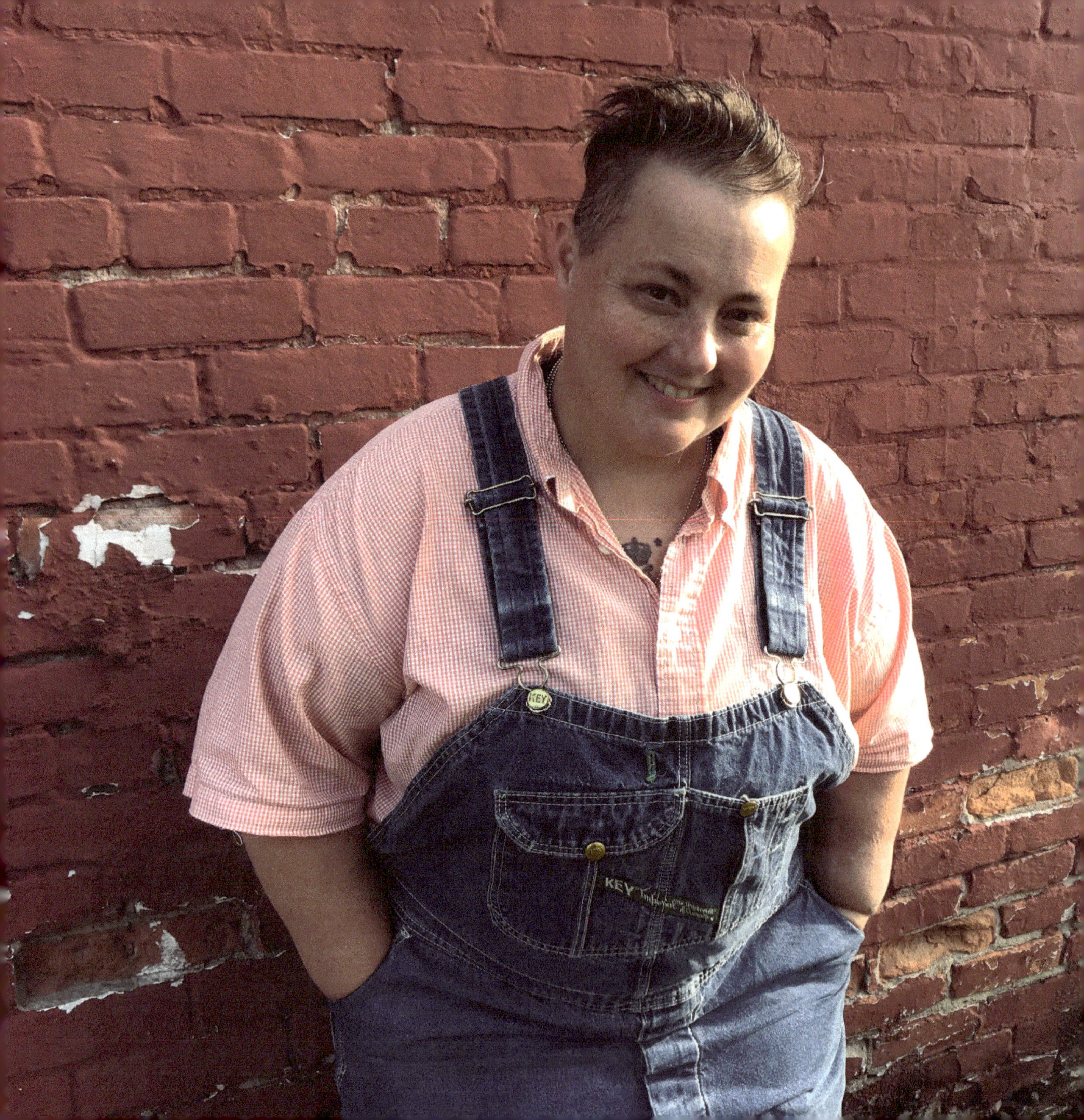

I am the youngest of seven children from a rural family, a family that was struggling and needed their last born to be cheerful and greet all manner of upheaval with, "Oh that's okay. I can deal with that."

Instead, when my mom was pregnant she said by the amount of commotion I made in her uterus she knew I was "a boy or heaven help us a girl." If she only knew how prophetic she was being.

Throughout childhood, my parents were extremely generous about my gender expression; my mom only made me wear a dress once a year for school photos. They were almost heroic in their acceptance of having a weird little boy/girl in rural Wisconsin in the 70s.

What didn't work in their strained-to-the-max life was my sensitive genderqueer heart. I got so upset when I heard about the clubbing of harp seals, I didn't sleep for two nights. When it rained and all the worms emerged onto the road, I would miss the bus to school in my futile attempts to pick them all up and place them back on the grass so that they wouldn't get run over.

This was inconvenient behavior from someone in a girl package, but from someone in a boy package it was unthinkable.

My dad reminded me "boys don't cry" almost every day.

In adulthood, I ran away to be queer, always in big cities. I finally settled in Brooklyn and learned from the emotionally capable (mostly) queer folks around me that sensitivity is a personality characteristic, not a character flaw; I notice when my partner is feeling stressed about her job or a friend has a bad day.

The only people I knew growing up who wore overalls were the stoic rural men of my family. For years I avoided wearing them. But the more I came to value my own way of being masculine, the more I could embrace my rural roots. Wearing these hand-me-down overalls from another butch in the community is my way of saying, "Sometimes boys do cry."

KELLI DUNHAM is the genderqueer ex-nun storytelling nurse comic so common in modern Brooklyn. Kelli has appeared on Showtime and the Discovery Channel, the Moth Mainstage, the Cinderblock Comedy Festival, the Risk podcast, the Gotham Storytelling Festival, and nationwide at colleges, prides, fundraisers, and even the occasional livestock auction. Kelli was nominated as a 2105 White House Champion of Change (*not under the current administration*) for her work as the co-founder and producer of Queer Memoir, NYC's longest-running, most super earnest LGBTQ+ storytelling event.

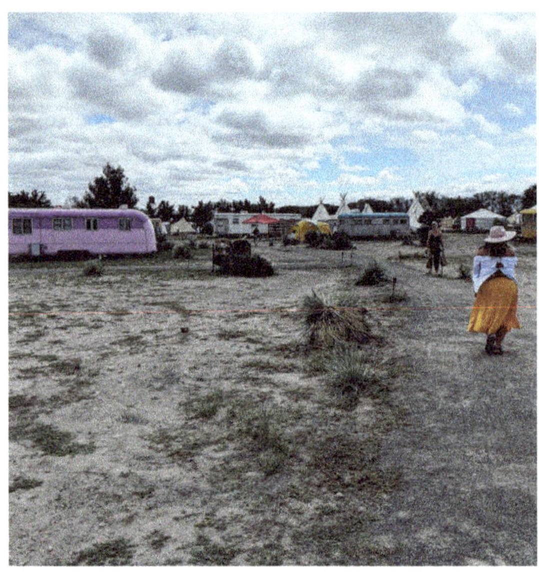

AARON DEUTSCH writes in praise of homonormativity and celebration of all things "extra." His work has appeared in *Scalawag Magazine* and *Willows Wept Review* and is inspired by the people he loves.

DELRAE WALKING

Once I hated my body so much I treated it like an immigrant
to the clean marbled colonies of my mind. I sent rules and notes
down on pigeons and white kites.

Then I built a cocoon from those papery edicts, and scrawled over them
in the reptilian language of lung and limb, the ellipsed history
of human evolution. The hard, sluggish climb from tarry murk
up the escarpment. The ingress into daylit spaces. All this,
with no legs to stand on.

I emerged in my body, and followed a bare-breasted witch woman,
blond as oleander, gowned in yellow songbirds, into the desert,
watched her honor her sex and wear it like pink mink. Upraise her protest
on the queer breezes blowing over the bones of Crazy Horse
and Morning Dove.

We cut our feet on brown scorpidium and wove blood
into rugs of dried columbine and bantam nodes that hung,
in this ruddy place, like napping bats, keen no more to search
for our place to stand.

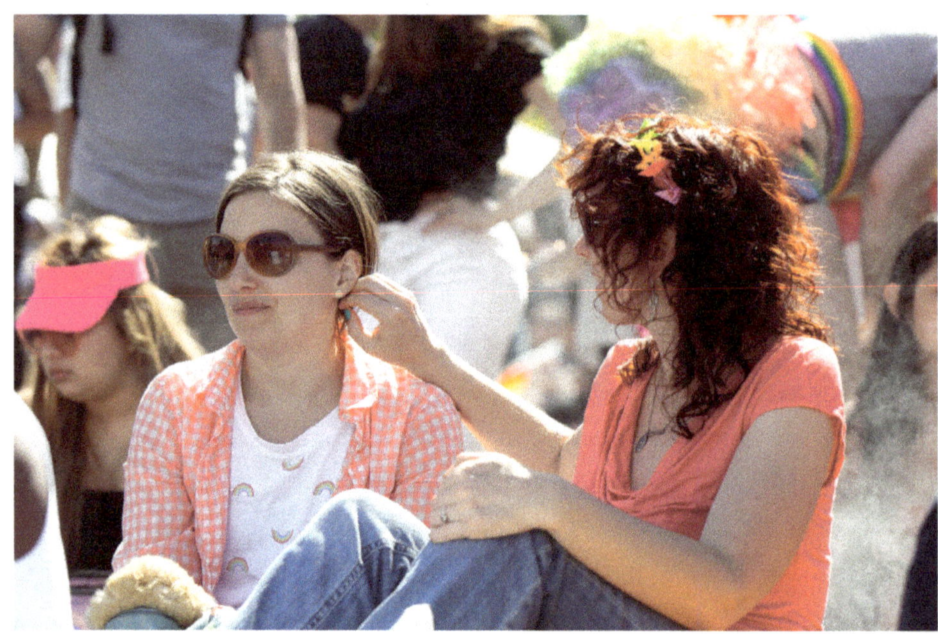

PENELOPE GAY DANE lives with her partner in Sacramento, California, where the pollen is plentiful and the stray cats let the squirrels run wild.

HALF BOUGHT, HALF WON

Is there anything more queer than hair? I was queer before I became a lesbian, my hair tangled. Ringlets. Frizz halos. In 1992, I was 17 and my friends and I rode the subway 45 minutes, walked through the biting Boston wind to the kink shop in Central Square. Locked in a glass counter next to the sex toys, squat cylinders of hair dye beckoned. I left with Apple Green, tucked in a plain paper bag.

In the suburbs, our eyes stung from drug store bleach. We ruined towels, stained bathtubs, angered our mothers. The kids at high school shouted, why is your hair green?

Because I like it. Because I do not belong here. I didn't say lesbian. I dyed my hair, slunk past lockers.

When your now is filled with loafers and Laura Ashley and rugby pullovers, you resist until you arrive at your queer future. You armor up for school with go-go boots and fishnets.

I live in my queer future. Now. I'm an eco lipstick lezbo. My last white sequin dress got blue gum on it.

In this photo, I sit at the 2019 Dyke March in Dolores Park, San Francisco. My hand brushes my partner Cara's neck. She wears gingham and rainbows. Hey, I whisper, Maggie's taking our picture.

My melon t-shirt is from a thrift store sale. Secondhand jeans. Henna for my hair.

We dykes and queers fill the park. The sidewalks. Shouting. Dancing. Cuddling. Sun. Music. Macramé. Sequins. Leather. Pastel unicorns pasted on platform boots.

Apple Green hair me never imagined a world with so many of us.

This picture is Cara and me. In the middle of it all. I folded the origami butterflies on my headband, burned my fingers on the glue gun. My necklace is half bought, half won. Joan d'Arc blazes on the pendant that was pressed into my hand at the Joan d'Arc parade in New Orleans. Next to the pendant hangs a rectangle. Small letters pressed into the silver. Warrior.

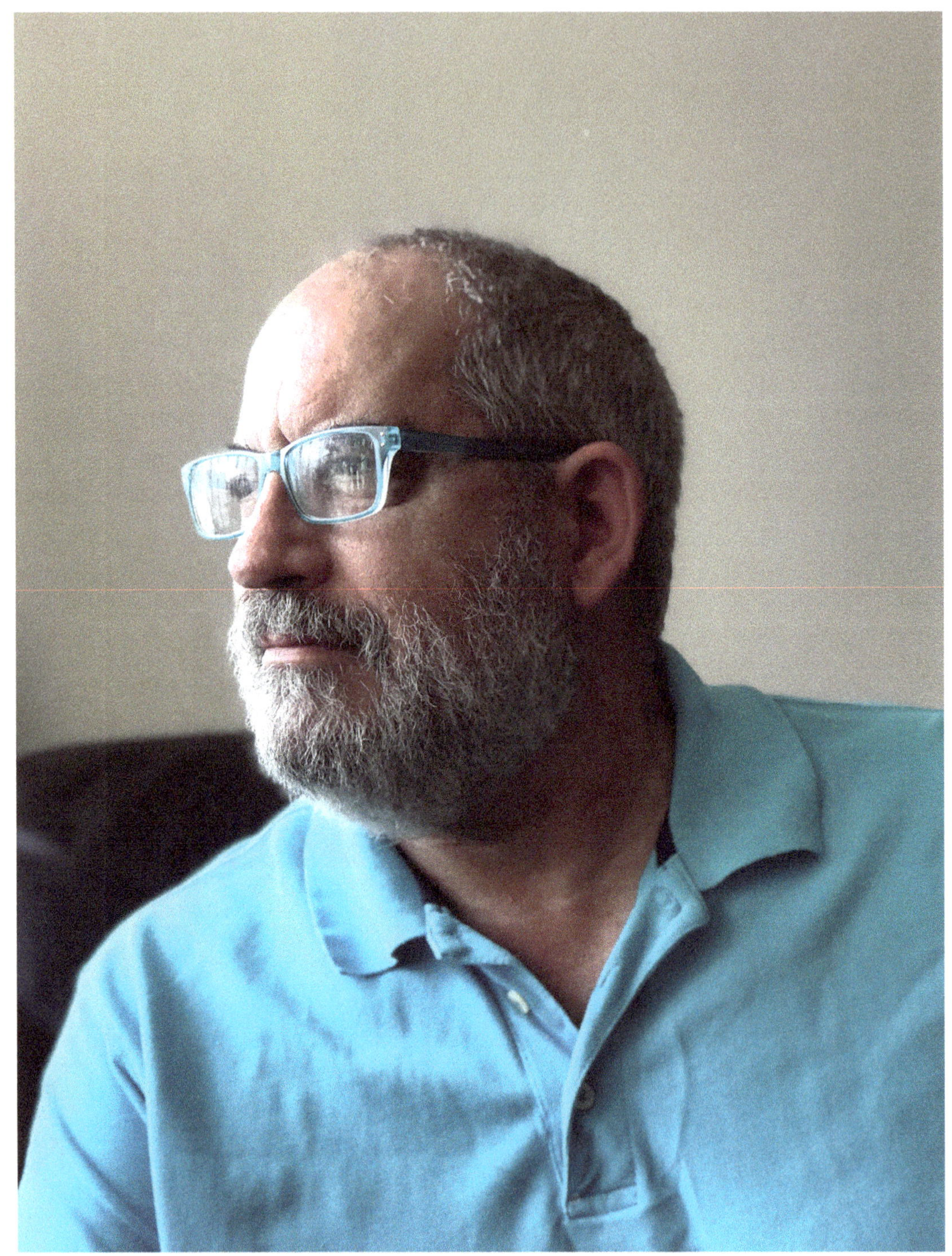

OPTICAL FASHIONISTA

It was not my intention to become an optical fashionista, I just wanted to stop losing my glasses . . . and walking into things.

I'm extremely near-sighted, and am only able to see clearly in an area from three to nine inches from my nose, and was constantly losing my glasses. I've *literally* gone for three days without being able to see a damn thing because I couldn't *see* where I'd put the damned things. The solution came to me while perusing the Zenni Optical catalog online. I ran across a pair of frames that was colored something along the lines of whatever the hell they used in the original *Star Trek* series whenever they needed to trot out the Romulan Ale—sort of a carbonated Windex in hue.

So I ordered them, and boom-chica-boom, they arrived. Unfortunately, not five minutes after I'd put them on my face, I had to scratch my nose and put my gawd-awful colored glasses onto a book (and I'm not making this up) with a cover that matched the specs perfectly.

It's not an entire loss; I have a polo shirt almost the exact same gawd-awful color and whenever I wear them together (which I've never knowingly done on purpose), I get compliments up the core and down the back. (The thing of it is, I often just grab the cleanest polo shirt in my closet without paying attention to if it has holes in it or the color).

I do a fair amount of copy editing and I needed something to wear when working on the computer. Since I failed with my gawd-awful frames I just looked at my ex and said, "I give up, you pick, and go hog wild." Which is how I ended up with the 60s-chic white frames.

The third pair? They're just an old pair that I keep around because I'm still misplacing my glasses.

DAVID CUMMER is a long-time Minneapolis resident and has written for radio, television, and various LGBTQ+ publications, and has appeared in *QDA: A Queer Disability Reader*, *RFD*, and *Lovejets*.

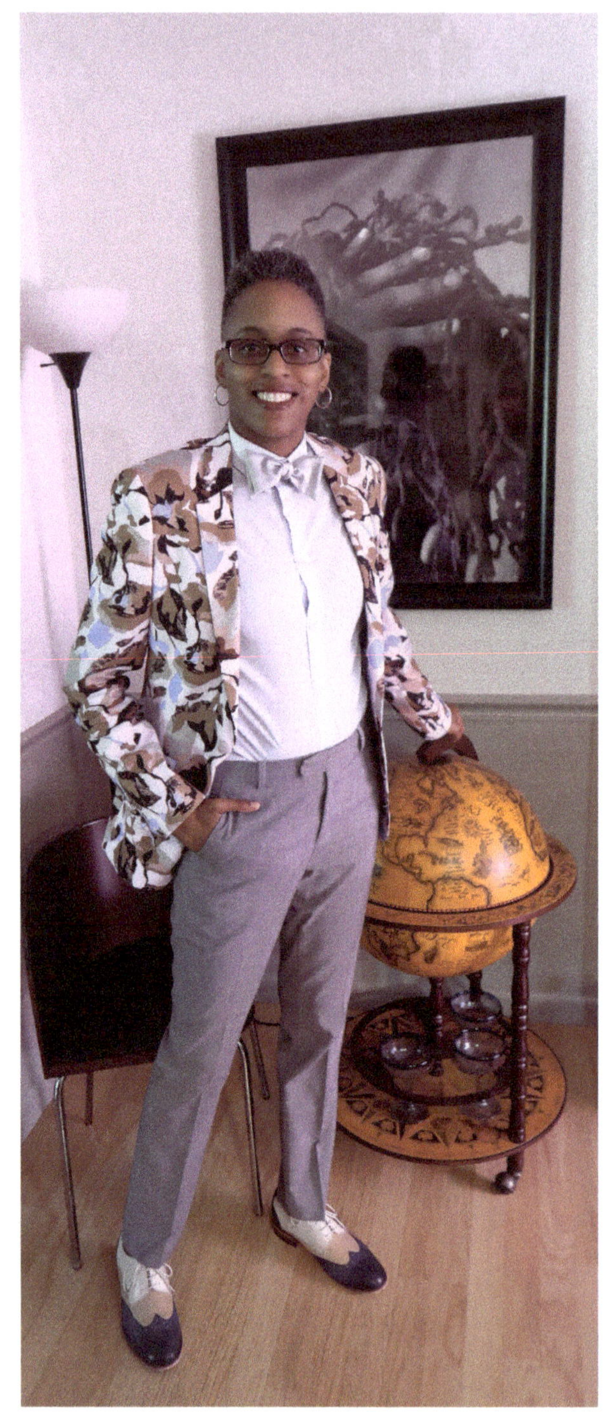

THE INHERENT QUEERNESS OF SELF-TYING

It took five aggravating attempts before I finally fumbled through a crudely shaped bow tie. At the time, I couldn't find anyone on YouTube who looked like me (black, queer cis-woman) creating tutorials for tying bowties. It matters more than one would realize.

Although the clothing industry is finally catching up to the undeniably queer fashion industry, it has been slow to budge from the sizing template for traditional menswear. And so, standard neckties are between fifty-six and fifty-eight inches in length and correspond to neck sizes of 16 to 17.5 and body heights between 5'11" and 6'3". My neck and body are about three inches shy of this "standard." So when I watched the (mostly white) men demonstrate their perfectly executed bowties, it was without any necessary adjustment beyond this standardized body type.

For those of us whose childhood rites of passage did not include learning how to tie neckwear, or who are still in childhood, or in need of a standardized uniform accessory, there are pre-tied options. Pre-tied neckwear is available in many styles for those who require accommodation. Dapper & Urban is a wonderful example of queer-made selections. Because pre-tied bows are often used for uniforms and for children, at times they appear more novelty than classy. This is a distinction of taste; yet learning to tie neckwear is a necessary skill for the dapper queer.

Self-tying allows for flexibility in fit and the shape for bowties, which can alternately appear too large or small depending on the neck they adorn. Similarly, learning a variety of knots for neckties (the Eldredge is my favorite) that use more of the material creates a custom fit for various body types as well as event occasions. As such, the act of tying neckwear often is the first step of "queering" the accessory.

M. SHELLY CONNER is an Assistant Professor of Creative Writing at the University of Central Arkansas. She is the creator of the *Quare Life* web series and her debut novel *everyman* is forthcoming from Blackstone Publishing (2021).

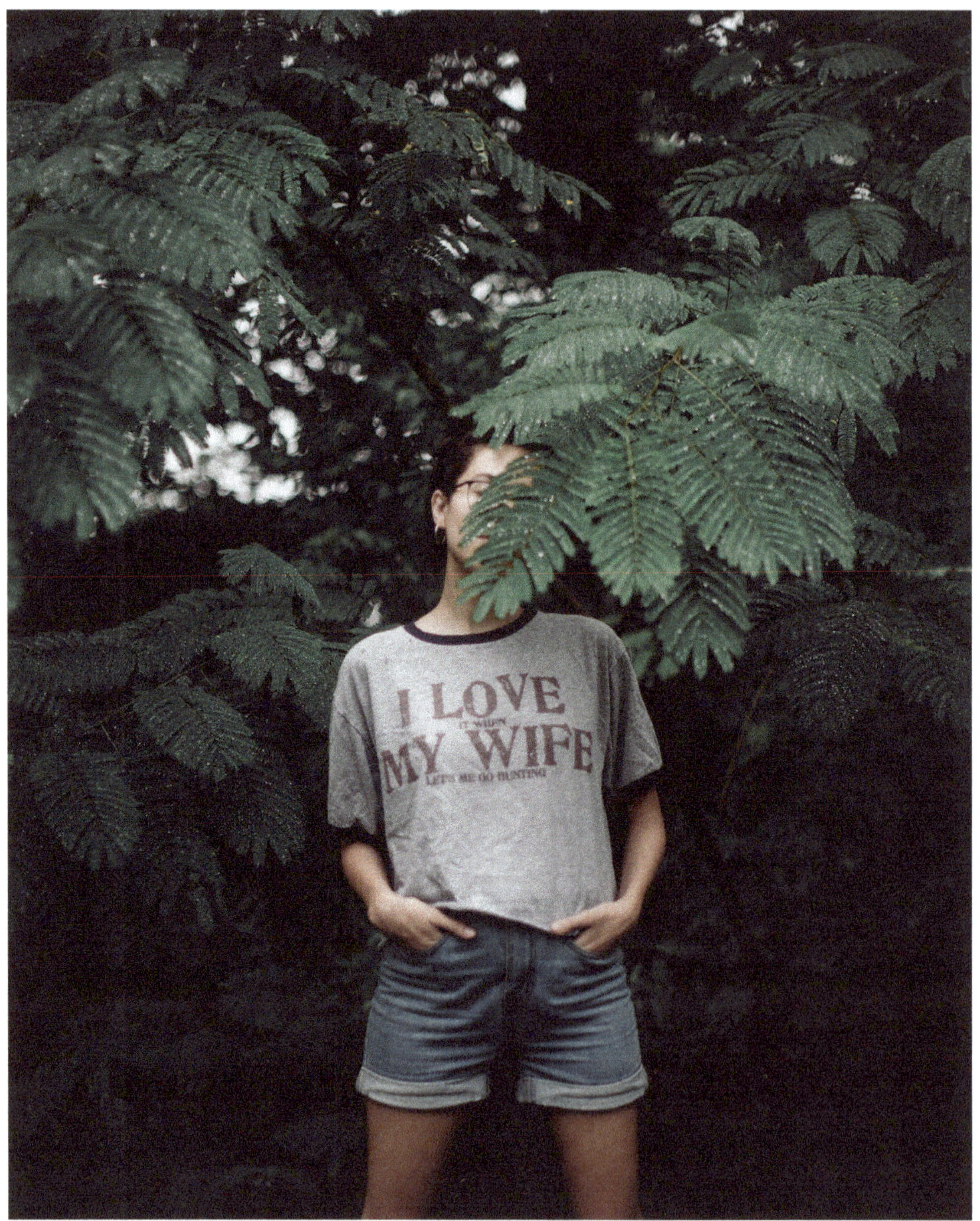
I LOVE
IT WHEN
MY WIFE
LETS ME GO HUNTING

I found this shirt at a thrift store a couple months ago that reads, "I LOVE it when MY WIFE let's me go hunting." It's gray with atrocious, rust-colored lettering, and "lets" is spelled incorrectly. It is, by all accounts, a bad shirt. It was too ridiculous to pass up, so I took it home, cropped it, and wore it the next day. I love that this painfully hetero, gender-role-affirming shirt becomes queer on me. And it makes me feel bold: a nod to my younger self who couldn't even hint her identity to her closest friends.

Most of what I wear I find secondhand. Searching for clothes was one way I started learning to give myself permission to be. And now as a handful of my friends explore their genders, thrifting together or with each other in mind becomes a collaborative act of identity formation: of self-love and of affirming each other. My friend Lexi and I are notorious for hauling piles of clothes from Goodwill Outlets (where clothes are sold by the pound!) and divvying up the trove among our queer pals. Her partner has begun to love wearing skirts, so we keep an eye out for long florals they can wear with their favorite pair of Blundstones. We just found the perfect shorteralls for my partner, dark denim that hits just above the knee—a length she feels best in.

When I look at my closet, I remember the work that went into it. The bulky hiking boots I found and wore nonstop after my mom started making snide comments about my leg hair. A cowboy boot button down, left unworn in my partner's closet for months until I cut the long sleeves and we had to fight each other to wear it that summer. Sifting through the masses to find the spectacular and the affirming feels not unlike that queer adage about chosen family. No one falls into their own style nor a solid queer community passively. There's a real effort behind choosing our people and continuing to choose them each day.

CLAIRE COMEAUX is a poet from Lafayette, Louisiana, currently living in Little Rock, Arkansas.

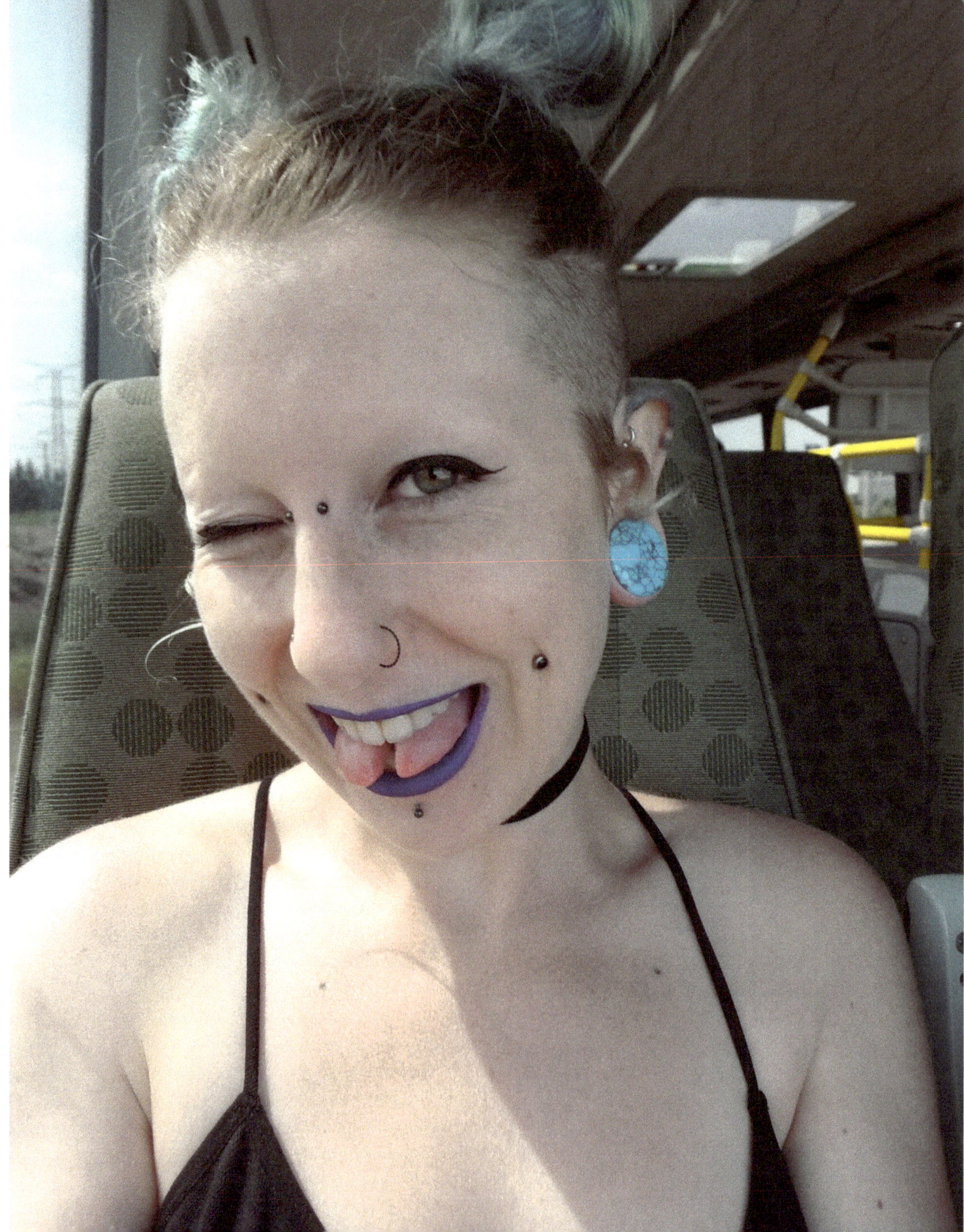

My choice of piercings, tattoos, and other body modifications were really one of my earlier choices in fashion statements. I currently have 17 piercings with 7 black ones on my face and I feel like I look more like myself with them. It's technically a lot of piercings, but the way they sit and look really compliments my face. I've also stretched my ears different sizes, shaved my eyebrows, and split my tongue, all of which help me feel more at home in this otherworldly body that I don't want people to read as solely "female." (I'm queer and non-binary, so that just won't do). It's been a journey though, with 12 of my earlier piercings not making the cut to stick around. Other body mods I've had done are tattoos, with about half of them being done on myself by myself. I love wearing art and using such a permanent form to enhance my being. I've tattooed my armpit with pretty diamonds and my belly with a lotus flower as I used to not find these parts of my body lovely, but now I love showing them off because I just added simple lines and changed how I feel about them completely. They are so beautiful, and art, fashion, and modifications are limitless in the good they can bring people.

SIMONNE CLOUT is a queer non-binary Aquarius studying biology and genetics who loves odd music and style.

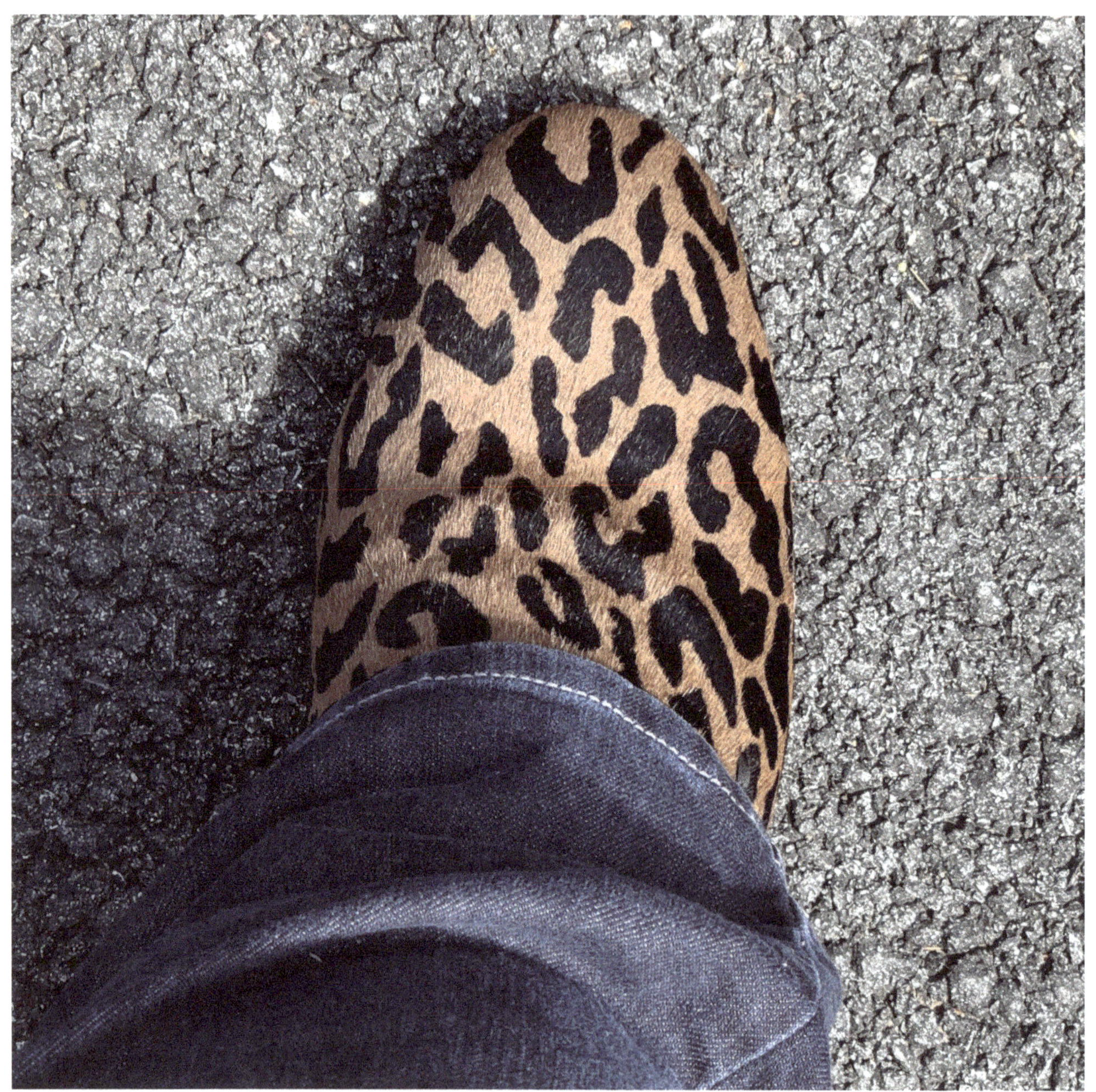

THE HUNT

I was knee-deep in casual shoes at DSW when I spotted them from across the room, simply by chance: a pair of leopard print slip-ons to end all others. Even several aisles away, I could tell these were true beauties. As soon as I saw them up close, I melted. I slipped the right shoe on and examined how my foot looked in them. Being queer, fat, and fashionable, shoes are but one of a limited way I can express my sexuality. I am ultra-conscious that the clothes I wear to showcase my queerness are not mistaken for Bozo Cosplay. So many styles and trends can go horribly wrong. But when I looked down at the shoe on my foot, it sang to me. It was as if I were Dorothy, spellbound by the Ruby Slippers magically appearing on my feet. I knew I must have them.

As with any great hunt, the chase was not quite that simple. When I brought the leopard shoes to the counter, the cashier found they were mismatched in size. In the thrill of the chase, I had never tried on the left! The clerk prowled about, looking for the matching size, but the left leopard was elusive.

The next week I went to one of the other DSWs several towns over. The day was ominous, and as I began the hunt once more, the skies opened and the rain poured down. But I reached the store and made my way through the jungle of aisles. I cut in and out in search of the men's section, finally finding the correct row. I held my breath as I scanned the size on the boxes, letting out a gasp when I saw them, Leopard Print Shoes, Size 12. I quickly slipped them on, one foot at a time, and admired them in the mirror. Stylish. Queer. Mine!

BRIAN CENTRONE is a writer and a teacher. He has an M. A. in Costume Studies from New York University. His research focused on menswear, where he looked at the role gender, sexuality, and masculinity played in men's eighteenth-century breeches, as well as the impact nineteenth century anxieties about dress and sexuality had on the persecution of Oscar Wilde. Brian's interest in the developments that occurred to men's suits during the end of the nineteenth century led him to research the origins of the trouser crease for his thesis.

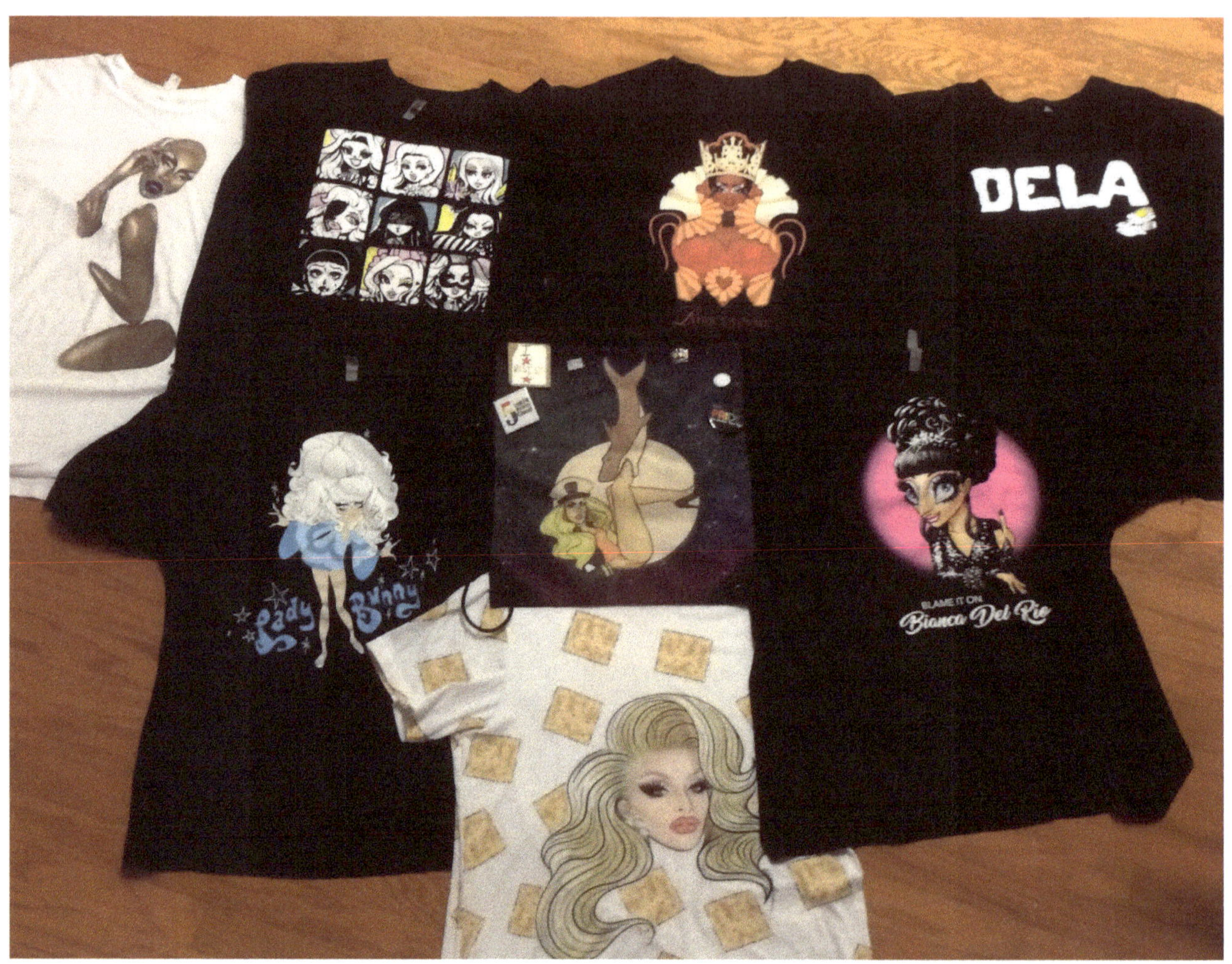

ALEX CARRIGAN is an assistant editor with the American Correctional Association. He has edited and proofed the anthologies *CREDO: An Anthology of Manifestos and Sourcebook for Creative Writing* (C&R Press, 2018) and *Her Plumage: An Anthology of Women's Writings* from *Quail Bell Magazine* (forthcoming 2019). He has had fiction, poetry, and media reviews published in *Quail Bell Magazine*, *Life in 10 Minutes*, *Realms YA Fantasy Literary Magazine*, *Mercurial Stories*, *Lambda Literary Review* and the forthcoming anthology *Stories About Penises* (Guts Publishing, 2019). He currently lives in Alexandria, Virginia.

DRAGGED OUT

It wasn't until my early adulthood that I realized part of my queer identity had always been present in an unrealized love of drag. I had been fascinated by drag queens as a kid, but because I had such little exposure to it growing up, I didn't realize how I loved it. When my friend Victoria showed me *RuPaul's Drag Race* back in college, everything suddenly made sense. My queer identity could finally pop out of a box like Shangela because I connected to the subversive and irreverent art form with my own character.

It was hard to see live drag until I moved to Washington D.C. in 2017. There, I realized I had finally found a proper drag community, with drag brunches and queens on Pride floats. Because I was in a major city, I could finally go to venues that had queens from the show performing. As a good Judy, I made sure to start buying merchandise at these shows, acquiring a decent collection of t-shirts of some of my favorite drag queens. I felt blessed to see Shea Couleé, Kim Chi, Latrice Royale, BenDeLaCreme, Bianca Del Rio, and Miz Cracker live, as well as drag legends like Lady Bunny, so I had to take some part of the shows home with me.

The centerpiece of my drag collection is a drawstring bag depicting my all-time favorite queen, Katya Zamolodchikova. My friend Rachel sent me the bag as part of a birthday package, and I'm so grateful for it. Katya helped me deal with a lot of anxiety and depression the year I started identifying as queer through her TV appearances and web shows, so just having a bag with her irreverent visage on it was one of the best gifts for my collection.

As someone who now has a *Drag Race* shirt for every week of Pride and a cool button-adorned bag to go with them, I am more confident expressing my queer identity through such talented and hilarious individuals, from whom I hope I can continue to draw inspiration.

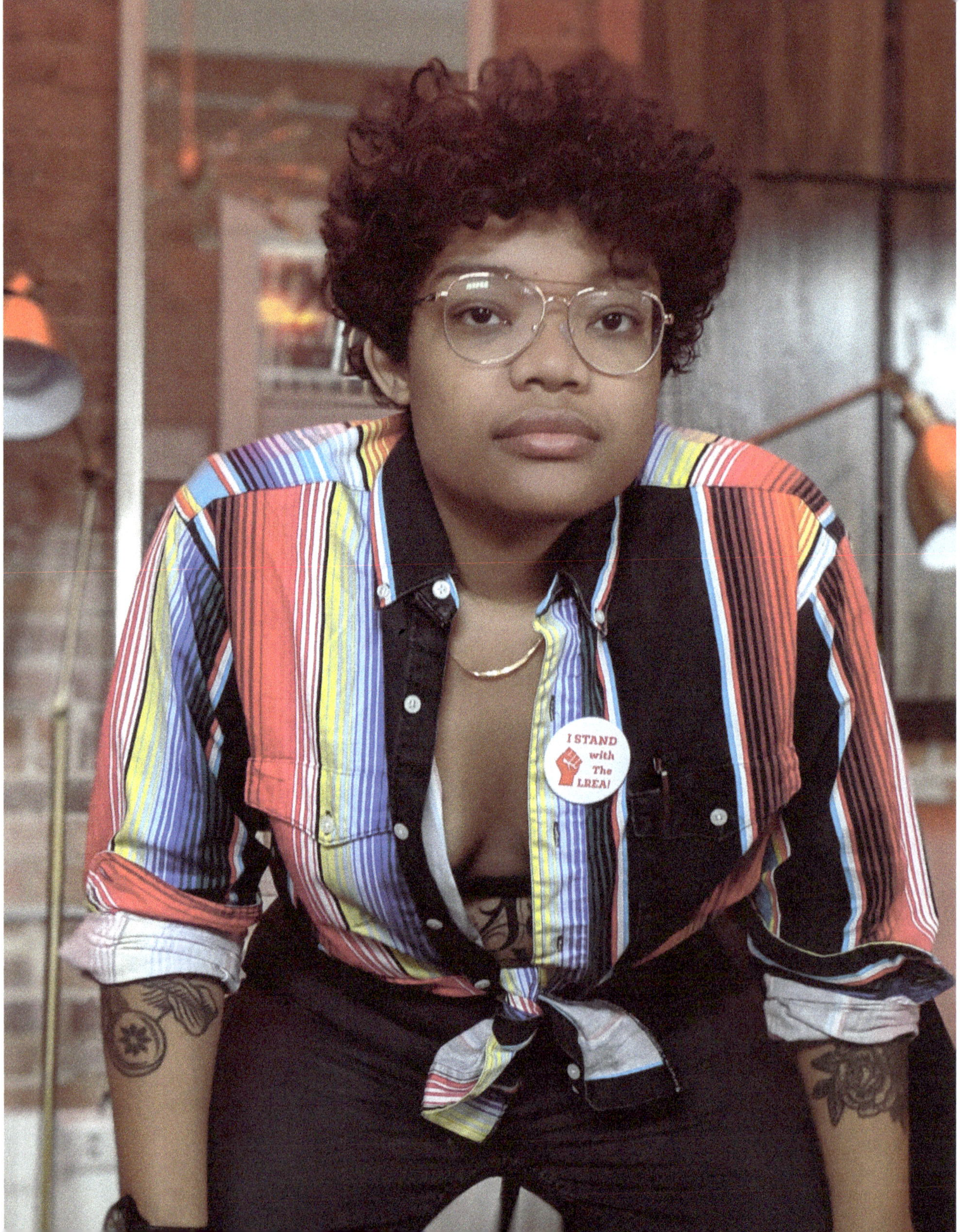
I STAND
with
The
LREA!

IT WAS HIS CHAIN

The chain is arguably the ultimate symbol of traditional Black masculinity. A gold chain is more than a valuable accessory: it is a family heirloom. It signifies a transition to manhood. It is a mark of independence and self-sufficiency that allows for significant purchases.

Plus, they look hard as hell.

I can't fully explain *why* the gold chain is iconic among heterosexual Black men, probably due in part to not having life experience as a heterosexual Black man. However, the most gender-affirming item of clothing I own is a gold chain inherited from my Tito Ronnie—a gay Filipino man. My memories of him exist through stories coaxed from my mother and gifted from his partner of 16 years, my Uncle Patrick. Tito Ronnie was Catholic. He was a tireless activist. He was also tied up in the traditional role he was expected to fulfill as the eldest son in a Filipino family.

I couldn't have been older than ten when we lost Tito Ronnie. I remember my mother sobbing when she received the news through the long-distance landline. I remember Uncle Patrick, a large bear of a Canadian, smoking outside with my father, a large Black man from South Carolina. They were both outsiders among the family. They get along well.

My gender identity exists outside of a binary. My ethnicity exists outside of a binary. When I am dressing myself—always intentionally—as to present as a genderqueer person, specifically a Black genderqueer person, I reach for this chain. As soon as it lies flat on my collarbone, I feel confident and strong. I feel like I have a right to claim and define Black masculinity for myself. This artifact of my queer family history doubles as a link to the ever-present chain around my father's dark brown neck. It reminds me of the chain my younger brother started wearing as he entered his twenties. My gold chain connects me to the multitude of communities contained in my existence.

Not to mention, I feel hard as hell.

JORDAN BUTLER is a Black Filipino who claims Little Rock as their home since 1998. They will not let you touch their hair.

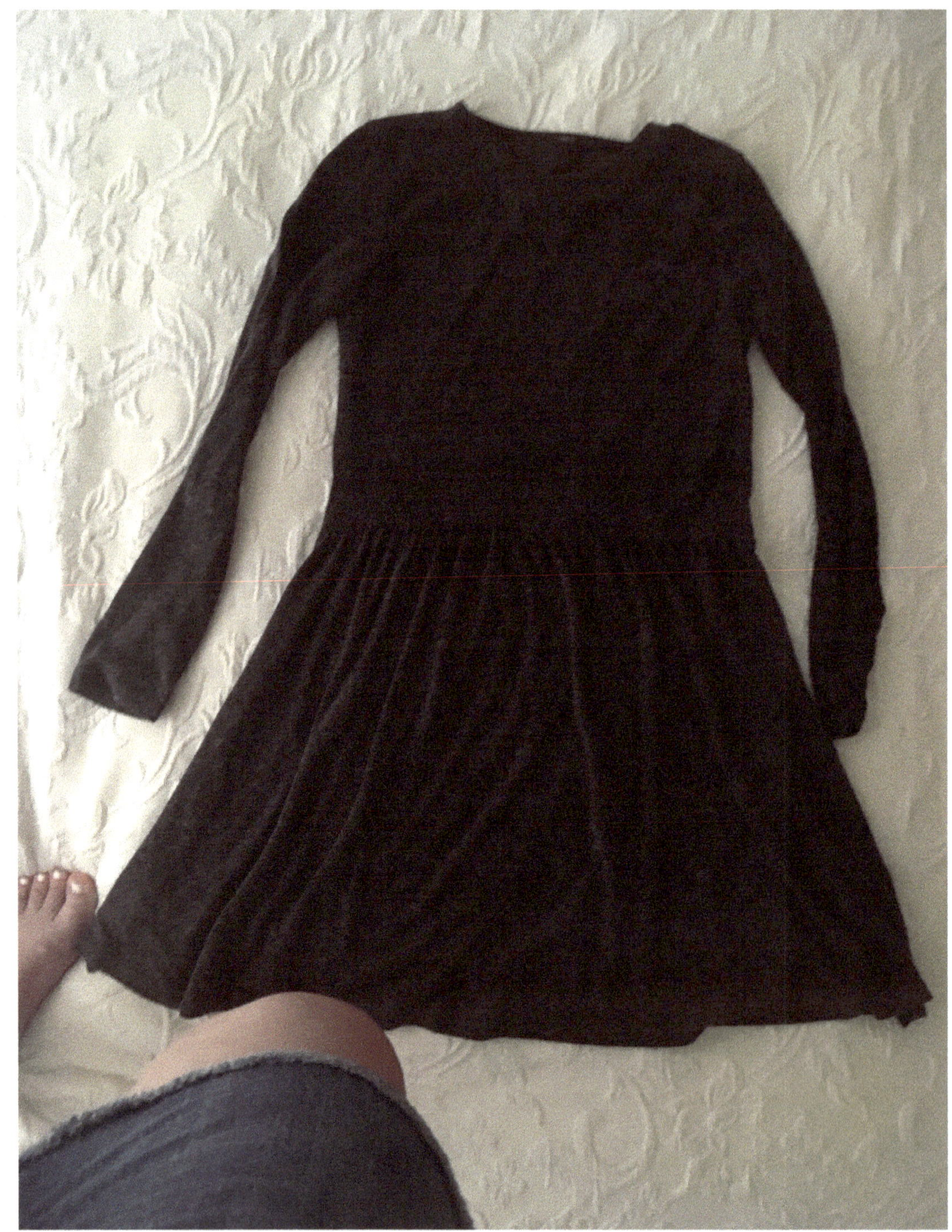

This is my wedding dress. I got married in Pike's Market in Seattle on March 1, 2014. I'm divorced now, which surprises me, though I would have put our odds at something like 40/60 that day. Okay, 30/70.

We were good together; it wasn't that. We didn't know each other well, and we were engaged about a year. We got married in Seattle because gay marriage was illegal in the state where we live, Arkansas.

My ambivalence about marriage was deep and intractable. I thought that my gay friends that were married were imitating straight people with their tuxes and gowns, their big parties and matching rings. That was not queer enough for me. Inside, though, I had daydreamed about a grand wedding celebration. I could see myself in a chic, ultra-feminine cream-colored designer gown in a chapel in New Orleans carrying a tumbling bouquet of red and yellow roses, or a delicate and enormously expensive clutch of lilies of the valley. The air would smell like lemon and petrichor, and the guests would have to shield their eyes from the glare of the visible-from-space cushion-cut diamond on my engagement band.

My real wedding dress is from ASOS, and it cost about fifty dollars. It is a skater style, fitted on top with a high waist and knee-length circle skirt. I chose gray for the dress, thinking it would echo the early spring Seattle weather, and I was not wrong. It kept me just warm enough that day, and I felt comfortable and super-cute, like the way I feel when I've snatched a polished look together for work and my skin and hair are behaving. I wore it with black tights, light gray boots, and a modest but lovely set of diamond and gold bands, identical to my wife's.

I've worn the dress five times since then, twice since my divorce. When someone compliments the way it looks I say, "I got married in this dress," in a light way, over my shoulder, and walk away before they can ask questions.

JANE V. BLUNSCHI holds an MFA in Fiction Writing from the University of Arkansas. She was a Lambda Literary Emerging Voices fellow in 2014, and her collection of stories, *Understand Me, Sugar*, was published in 2017 by Yellow Flag Press. Her work has appeared in *Paper Darts*, *SmokeLong Quarterly*, and *MUTHA Magazine*. Originally from Lafayette, Louisiana, Jane lives in Fayetteville, Arkansas.

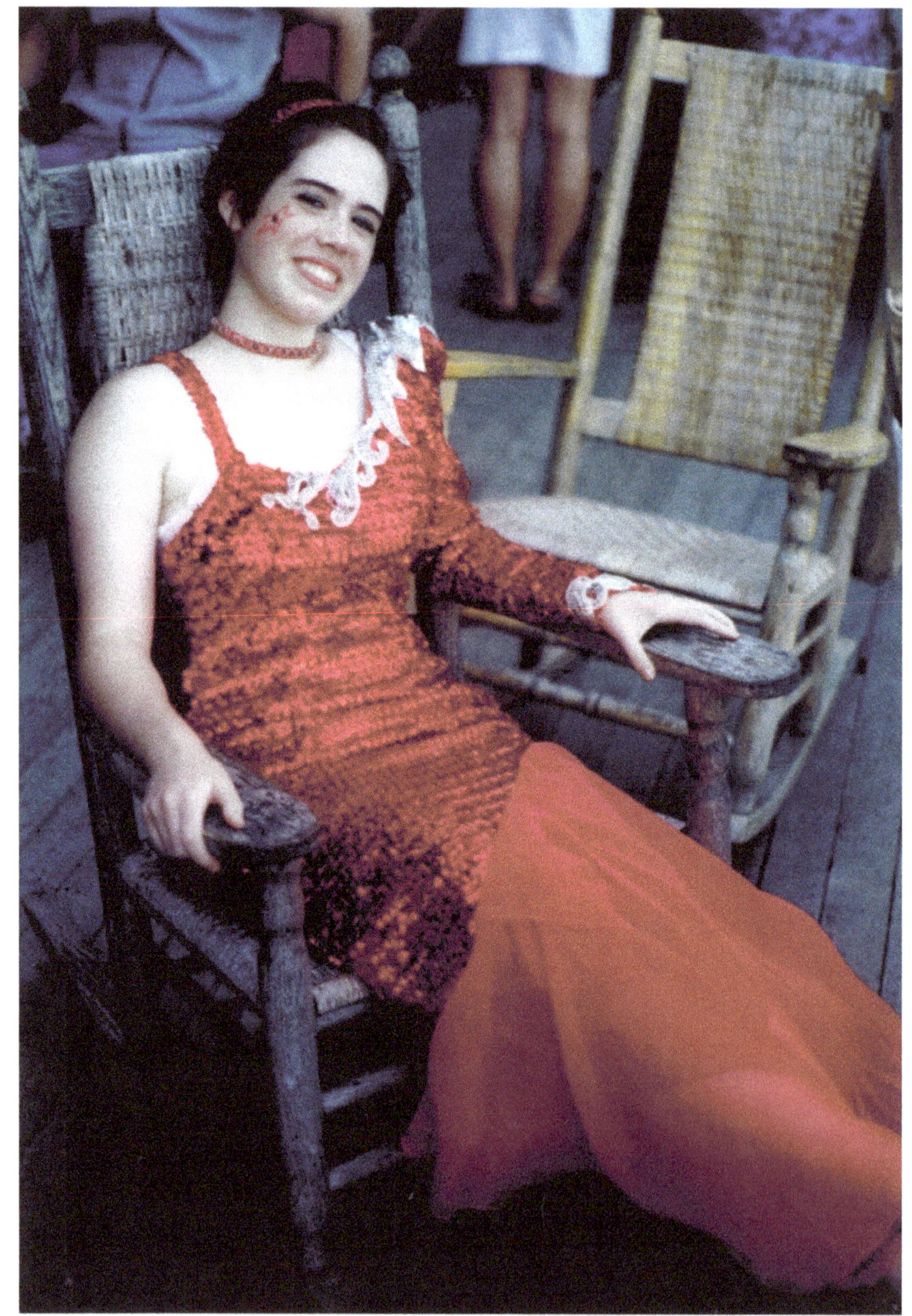

FIRECRACKER

At age fourteen, I had my first crush on a girl and I was obsessed with *The Rocky Horror Picture Show*. Often, I was so uncomfortable in my body I wanted to disappear, so I cut my hair pixie-short and wore button-up shirts, men's corduroys, and oversized hoodies. But with my curves and long eyelashes, I didn't look androgynous in the way I wanted to. And I was bullied at school for being queer, although I hadn't come out.

When I couldn't disappear, I tried instead to sparkle as brightly as possible, to become so visible that my glamor and eccentricity were a shield. I learned to put on self-confidence like a costume.

My older brother and I bought our clothes at thrift stores around Baltimore, which were a gold mine of glittery fashions in the '90s. On one trip I got a purple sequin cocktail dress; on another, a silver lamé shirt.

The most glorious outfit we found was the Firecracker dress—an evening gown dripping with red sequins, with silver-and-white curlicues at the neckline and wrist. Above the knee, the sequins ended on a bias and translucent red chiffon trailed to the ankles. I wore it only once, to my first year at a Unitarian Universalist summer camp on Star Island. We all dressed up for the last night.

There's a winding staircase in the Victorian hotel on the island. I got dressed and walked down that staircase alone, and at the landing I stopped in awe. Through the west-facing window, the setting sun illuminated my dress and reflected tiny red lights to shimmer on the ceiling, the walls, and the white lace curtains. When I moved, a galaxy of ruby stars moved with me.

My friend Alice took this photograph that night. She has a talent for capturing people's personalities. I was painfully self-conscious about the shape of my body, the way my skin was breaking out. But when she snapped the picture, all I saw was how brightly I sparkled, how happy and confident I looked. It seemed possible this brilliant version of myself was real.

ELIZABETH HART BERGSTROM is a queer, disabled writer of fiction, nonfiction, and poetry. Her work appears in *The New York Times*, *Post Road*, *Catapult*, *The Offing*, *Fourteen Hills*, and elsewhere. Photo by Alice Fawn.

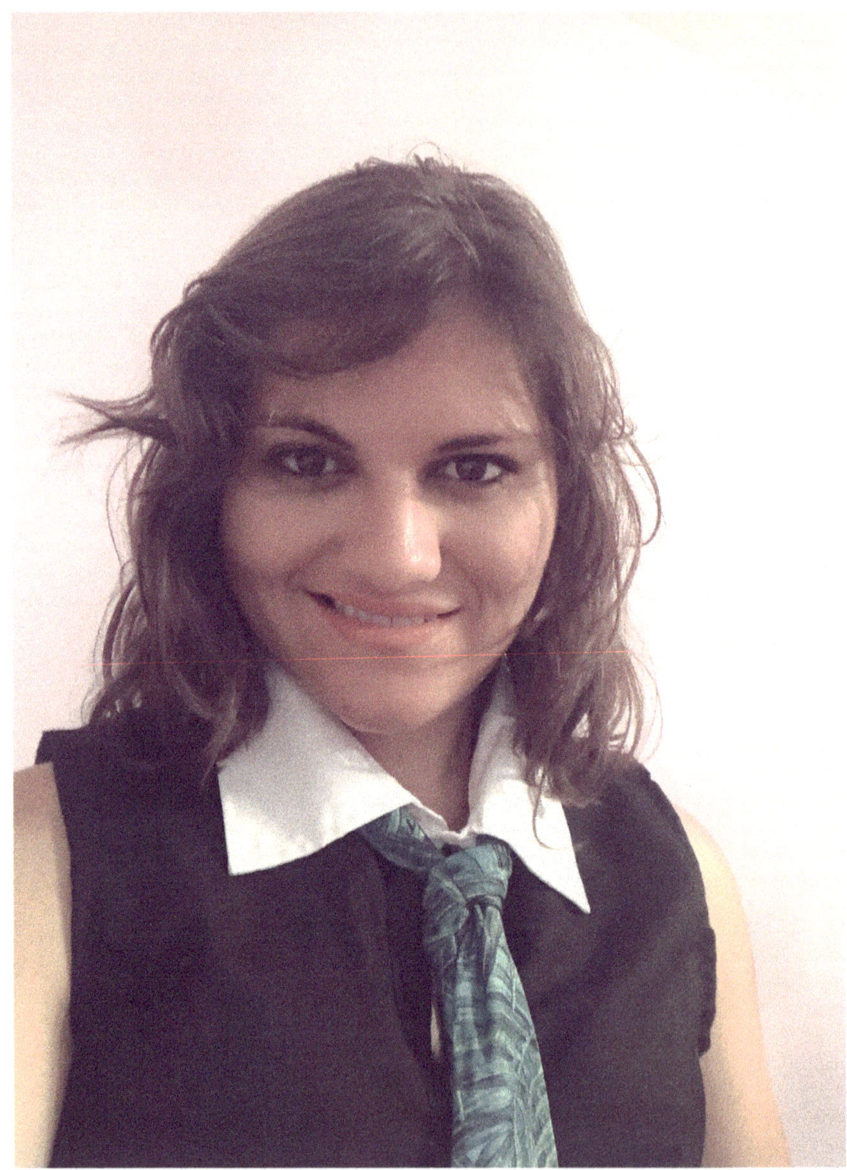

CLAYRE BENZADÓN is a second-year MFA student at the University of Miami and Broadsided Press's Instagram editor. She has been published by *The Acentos Review*, *SERIAL Magazine*, *HerStory*, and other lit magazine / journals, is forthcoming in *Poetry Breakfast*, and was recently awarded the 2019 Alfred Boas Poetry Prize for her poem "Linguistic Rewilding."

DAPPER

I sit alone
in my room, observe
my slanted, framed self
displayed in a dress.

My arms glint awkward
beneath thin
straps of black satin,

skirted fabric pressing
knees, flabby at the waist.

See, I prefer a certain type
of tenderness, a vested mid-

riff loose-fit uncovering,
the kind where I openly

settle down in baggy pants,
roll up my sleeves,

all accentuation of muscle,
collar, adjusted with a necktie, balancing out unrestrained

hang of a suit—how it stands
so easy this way, lets my
body become unbound.

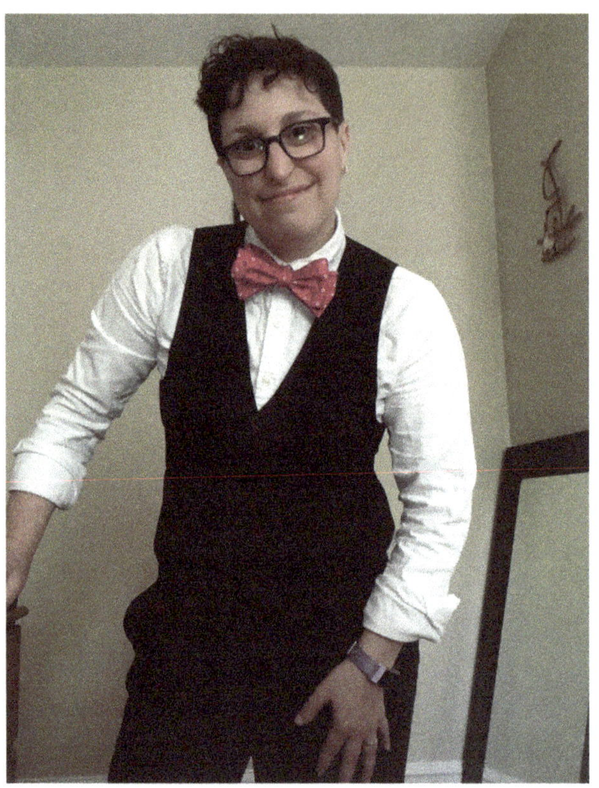

HANNAH BAKER-SIROTY lives with her family outside of Boston, where she runs the undergraduate writing program at Pine Manor College. She spends her summers out of the classroom—and her vests—doing odd jobs around her house, writing, and adventuring with her two young children in search of the best ice cream in New England.

WAISTCOAT

Lock me in—not too
tight, but—just enough.

Not completely held in, really,
is what I mean. In this

I feel more
put together

than ever. This is not a revolution,
even though tonight it feels

like one. I mingle
with gin-and-tonic, alive.

I am who you think I am.
It's okay, I admit it—freely.

I'm invested in causes and
move like the person you think I am.

I always have.

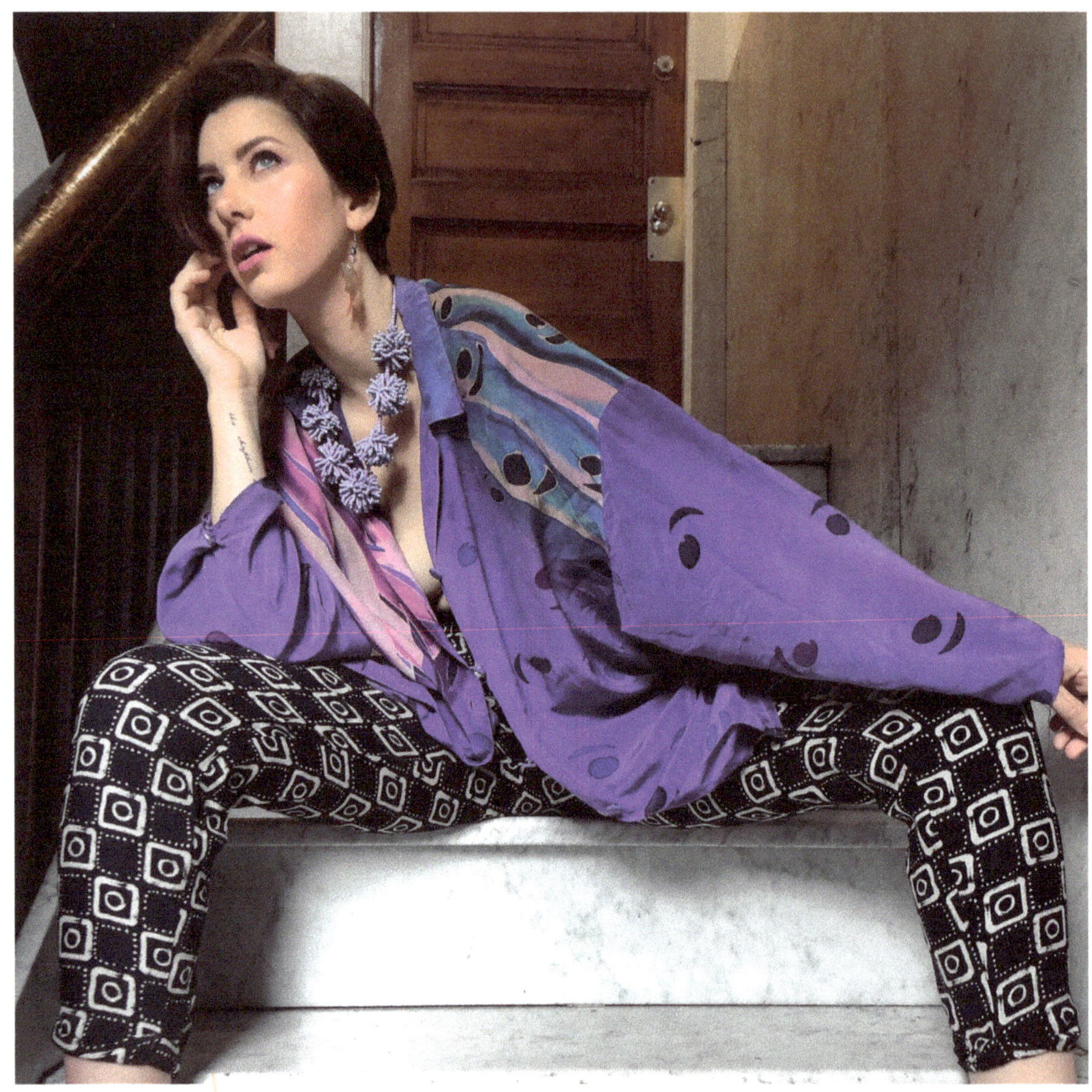

RUBY BACHEMIN is a wanderlusting, color obsessed, queer movement artist with an old soul. She has lived in and traveled through more than 20 countries street performing, acting, hula hooping, and burlesquing, seeking to find and spread joy in all aspects of life. She is based in her hometown of Cincinnati performing solo and as a member of the queer burlesque troupe Smoke & Queers. She aspires to help people fall in love with themselves and discover the beauty in life through liberating self-expression.

i am a tapestry
        woven in technicolor

   a mosaic of patterns and hues

full,   textured,   unapologetic
        in my vibrancy

i am   **dark** tones

     light tones

silk and burlap

at times   i am flashy
      i am rough

not always pleasing to the eye
     or to the touch

but i was not woven to please you.

My mother is an artist. My grandmother was a seamstress. Both are obsessed with color and fabric, a trait that did not evade me by a long shot. Clothing has always been a powerful form of self-expression for the women in my family. A tool to shatter the mundane. Simplicity has no place in our closets.

This blouse was made by my mother. Silk dyed in an array of cool tones in the years surrounding my birth. Clothes carry stories with them and this piece holds many. It is a symbol of the creativity and vivacity of my family, a memory of the style of art my mom created before it evolved to what it is today, a snapshot of the life she lived before me. It swaddles me on the days I feel insecure in my body, it dances on my skin when I want to stand out and show off.

It is femininity. It is androgyny. I experience humanity, but at my core I am so much more than that. That deeper part of me transcends time, space, gender, and any other limits constructed in this life. I feel that part of me deeply. It dictates how I identify and how I love. Human to human, soul to soul. As I experience this life, I experience womanhood. I experience the power, the magic, and the tragedy that comes with it, but it does not define me and I am learning more and more that it does not limit me.

With pieces like this, I can flow freely through masculinity and femininity. I can express the balance of these energies as they fluctuate within me. I can drape myself in a beauty that represents so much more than that which society expects from me. I can drape myself in me.

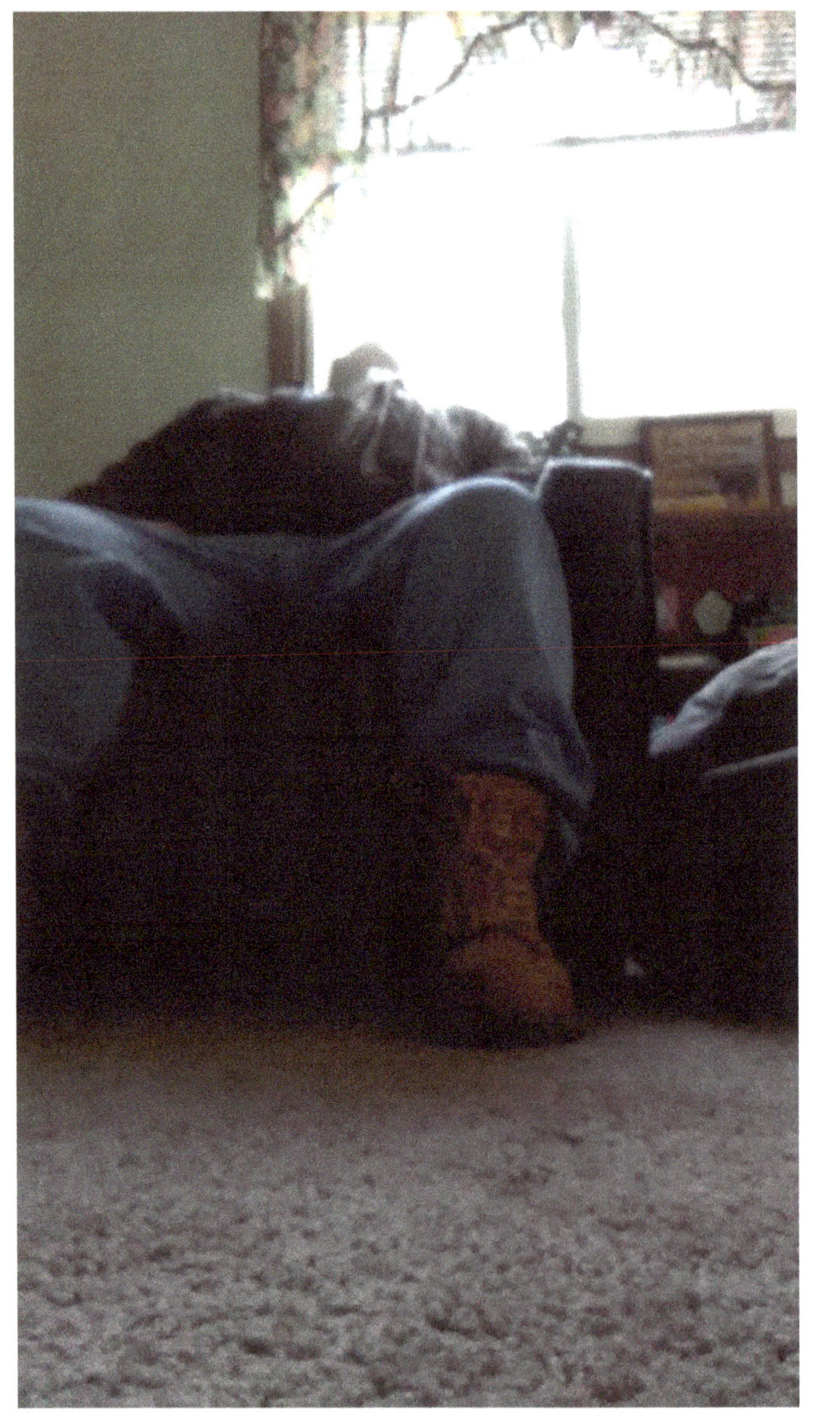

WORK IT MYTHOPOET

ten a.m., lemme rest, still dressed for the night & all evenings before,
for abraham stern, smoothing hide as i surrender handmedown jacket,
handover of gravel grime sweat to that of every man living, teeming,
loving dusk party kisses from enoch, poetry from ancient who touches
chinos to denim in whitman hand, cerulean thighs trembling like my
boy trachea, oil resistant soles backing up onto the toes of adam.

ULYSSES ARMEL is a white, working class, non-cis cub who sleeps
with men from Minnesota. His poems appear in other anthologies,
including *Exposure: Queer Masculine Sexuality* (Twin Cities Queer
Masculinity, 2017), *Lovejets: Queer Male Poets on 200 Years of Walt
Whitman* (Squares & Rebels, 2019), and *Manticore: Hybrid Writing
from Hybrid Identities* (Sundress Publications, 2019). He's usually also
wearing his "I Heart-Shaped-Bobber Fishing" hat and a gap tool on
the chain around his neck.

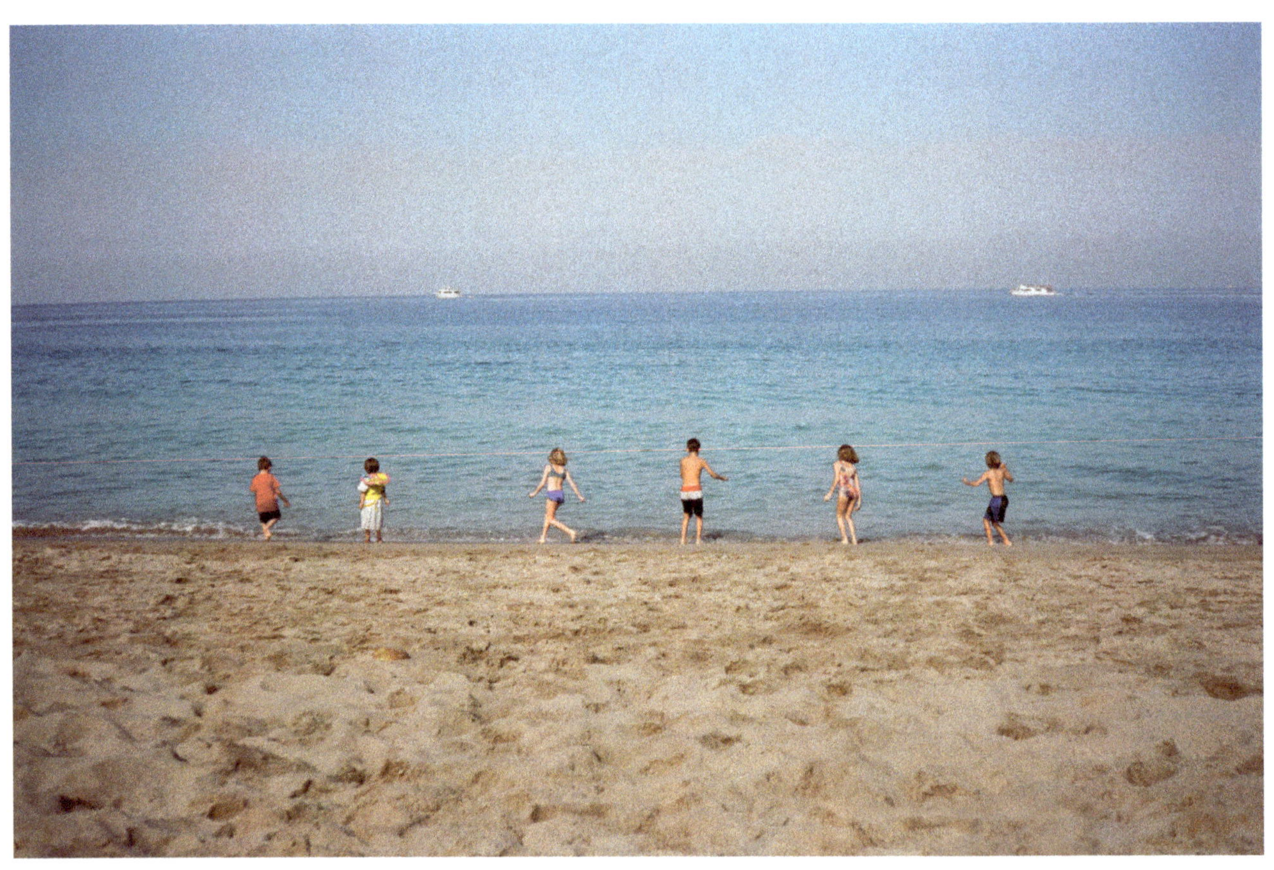

WESTON ANDERSON is queer person living in Portland, Oregon. Find them outside, playing DND, or writing.

TOMBOY IN A DRESS

There is a certain well-known photograph in my family. I, my two older brothers, and my cousins are all lined up on the beach. The photo looks staged, but it's not. The way my mom tells it, she was sitting on the beach, chatting with the other adults, when she looked up and there we were, all lined up facing the ocean. She grabbed her camera and captured the moment forever.

My cousins and my brothers all look as though they are about to jump into the advancing surf, but I am standing still, looking out into the vast expanse of the ocean. I also stand out because I am the only one wearing a life jacket, a pink number with Big Bird and the Cookie Monster printed on the back. And, it's not easily apparent at first, but I'm also wearing a white dress over my bathing suit. It was a simple white cotton dress with puffy sleeves and a few decorations done in white embroidery down the front. I remember the dress was displayed on a hanger in a store, high up near the ceiling. I thought it was the most beautiful dress I'd ever seen and I immediately begged my mom to buy it for me.

For as long as I can remember I've felt a strong duplicity in my gender. I tried to bury that feeling for so long, but after all these years it's still here. I am still that boy who is also not a boy. On one hand, I am more or less comfortable in my man's body, but on the other, I have never felt much like a man. To paraphrase author Jeannette Winterson, "I am a boy who is a girl who is a girl who is a boy." If I am a girl, I am a hairy girl. I'm the kind of girl who wears flats and not heels. And I'm the kind of girl who likes the idea of makeup in theory but hates the way it feels. If I am a girl, I am a tomboy.

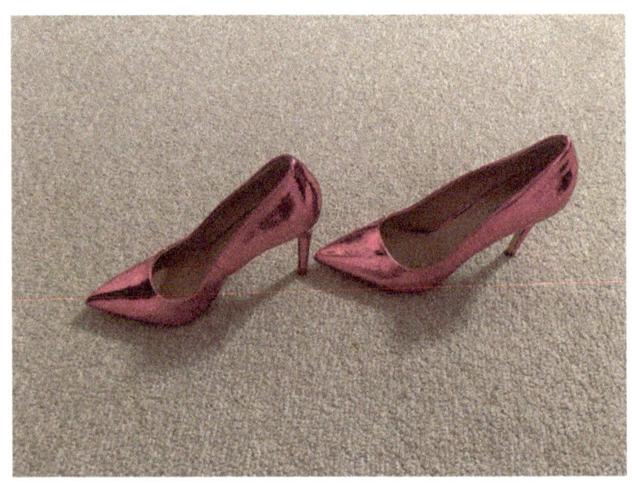

LISA NANETTE ALLENDER is an actor and writer who identifies as Bi. She has gotten to work opposite actor Robin Givens. Her work has been published in *Curve Magazine* and her poetry in numerous journals and magazines. Lisa enjoys cooking and baking. She loves rescuing dogs.

I remember wearing the most outrageous clothes. Long before I was *out*.

At 13 years old, I wrote to Eileen Ford at the Ford Model Agency. I sent her a school photo and my age, height, and weight. I was 4'11" and 80 pounds.

When I found the letter in our family's rural mailbox, with a postmark from New York City, I swooned. I floated back to my house, screaming about this letter, personally signed by agency head, Eileen Ford. "You are very pretty, Lisa. Since you are still quite young, should you reach our height minimum, please do contact me. Our minimum height requirement is 5'8".

I was addicted to fashion magazines. I loved seeing the latest trends and then *making them my own*. For instance, when tie-dye was hot, I'd wear bell-bottom pants and a hand-dyed *some-what*-matching long-sleeved shirt, instead of a halter. Suede fringed vests with bleached blue jeans.

I would wear lingerie as outerwear. Long before Madonna was "Like A Virgin," I was donning lacy bras and camisoles, wearing them with blue jeans and pencil-slim mini-skirts. For a long time, I thought my exhibitionistic attire was just that: exhibitionistic, a search for attention. At the same time, I was very insecure. I actually believed because I was of small build, and small-chested, that no one would notice me. I now know that wearing these clothes was my queer way of *owning my body*. I knew then that women were powerful. Hadn't I been attracted to my female teachers? Mrs. Farfante's very dark eyes, the way she tossed her head, her Cuban accent. Sister Maureen Michael's blue eyes, sand-colored brows, her heavy bosom trapped in a nun's unwieldy 1960s floor-length black and white habit. When the habits were modified a few years later, I got to see a few strands of her glorious sandy-brown hair peeking out from the new blue veils; the mid-length blue gabardine habit flowed over her globe-like breasts. I loved that she chose a boy's name as part of her chosen, *married-to-Christ* name. I remember being disappointed that she'd chosen it only because it was her family-of-origin's brother's name.

I attended parochial school from second through ninth grade, and when a new public school was being constructed just one mile from where I lived, my parents gave me a choice: did I want to attend public school? I already had a "good foundation," they said. I had one question: "Will I still have to wear a uniform?" "No, you can wear whatever you want; it's public school, Lisa." I imagined the mini-skirts I would wear, the midriff tops that would be called *sleazy*. I would get to buy platform heels, high heels!

Because it always begins with shoes . . . My obsession with high heels began that summer of 1972. My first pair of high heels were white platform shoes with a 3-inch heel. I graduated high school wearing 4-inch black high heels.

Decades later, these metallic fuchsia heels would scream from the shelves at my local Macy's, *"Buy me, wear me!"* I wear them with mini-skirts; I wear them with jeans. I wear them because they are ridiculously *feminine*. They are almost a parody of *femme*. They empower me, excite me.

They are my click-your-heels-together-and-you're-home shoes.

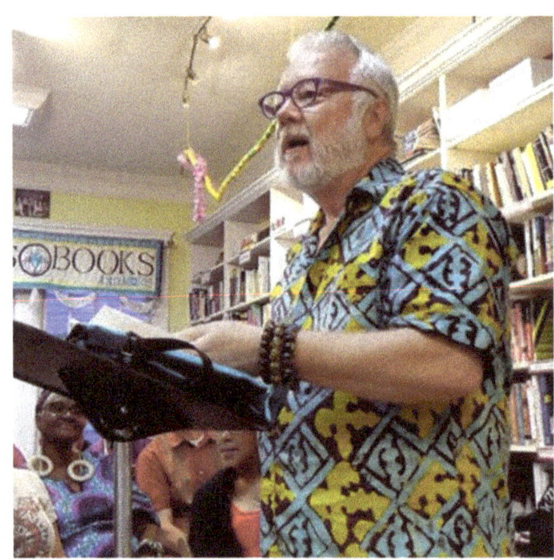

FRANKLIN ABBOTT is an original radical faerie and an LGBTQ+ organizer in Atlanta. He is a psychotherapist, poet, and musician.

I don't think much about clothes. I mostly wear what is comfortable. I can't tie a tie anymore and don't buy shoes that need polishing. I do think about clothes when I give public talks and readings. I have half a dozen shirts I have bought mainly on trips to Ghana that I like to wear because they are colorful and handmade, and the fabric dazzles with color and pattern. The shirt I am wearing in this photo is from my last trip to Ghana three years ago. My friend Nuumo helped me shop for it. There are some fancy shops in Accra, but the ones I like are pop up shops in Osu. They are on the street and that is where the shirt came from. It does not have a label that identifies who designed it, but I paid a little more for it because it has the Adinkra symbol for God on it, which makes it luckier. I am also wearing three bracelets of beads made for me personally by Nuumo. I love African beads and the ones in Ghana are especially lovely.

Nuumo Gblenfo III was an artist named Joe when I met him almost thirty years ago. When I returned to celebrate his 50th birthday, he was High Priest of the Ga people, a tribe of several million that live along the Atlantic coast of Ghana. His role is part pope and part chief justice for his people. For a while, he had a Judge Judy style show on one of the local TV stations. He dresses only in white and never wears shoes. People on the street know him and give him sway. He has a lot on his mind but relaxes when he is stringing beads together on a piece of elastic that he seals by striking a match that singes the ends together. The beads are heavy and full of Nuumo's good energy. Public readings are always exercises in vulnerability for LGBTQ+ people. Having some extra magic on hand makes the work a little more comfortable. Here I am reading at Charis Books (the old store location) in Atlanta.

Last Name	First Name	Instagram	Twitter
Yung	Airin	@airinyung	
Wozek	Gerard	@gerard.wozek	@gerardwozek
Wildner	Lucas		@wucas_lildner
Voltage	Max	@mxmaxpdx	@Max_Voltage
Volpert	Megan	@meganvolpert	@MeganVolpert
VanSickle	Al	@blushorbowtie	
Turner	Parrish	@TheParrishExperiene	@parrishturner
Tsai	Addie	@bluejuniper	@addiebrook
Tomsovic	Torey	@Toreytomsovic	
Thompson	Rowan	@ghostly_harmless	@rowbot_o
Taylor	Jules	@julestaylorwriting	
Stendhal	Renate	@renatestendhal	@renatestendhal
Sequoia	Anna	@SequoiaAnna	@SequoiaAnna
Sanders	Emma Brown	@ebs______	
Ryan	Lucy Hannah	@lucyhannahryan	
Russell	Lauren	@laureninred	
Romo	Randi	@TexMexLez500	@RomoTake2
Puels	Raina K.	@rainaaaaaaaaa	@rainakpuels
Pobo	Kenneth	@kgpobo	@KenPobo
Pechey	Ben	@benpechey	@ben_pechey
Nickel	Christiane	@scattermyashesataldi	
Napoles	Desmond	@desmondisamazing	@desmond_amazing
Mullen	Laura	@afteriwasdead	@afteriwasdead
Mitchell-Matsuyama	Renée	@matsuyama.michelle	@matsuyamarenee
Mirabella	Michel	@michel_mirabella	
Mettille	Noelle	@the_classyjunk	
McCutchen	Wryly T.	@wryly_xder	@Wryly_T
Martínez	Pablo Miguel	@pablomtz829	@pablito210
Mann	Jeff		@JeffMannAuthor
MacNeil	K. Ann	@kamacneil	
Leland	Kate	@Kate.Leland	@KateLelandPoet
Leifer	Liz	@25toleifer	

Last Name	First Name	Instagram	Twitter
Kojadinovic	Miodrag	@miodrag_kojadinovic	
Knight	Ferris		@ferris_knight
Kelley	Collin	@collinkelley	@collinkelley
Kashala	Tig	@mixx_kashala	
Kaplan	Bonnie S.	@bonkaplan	
Kamel	Nour	@screamlnour	@screamlnour
Kafarela	Brandon	@tooflako	
Jackman	Kyle	@kaijckmn	
House	Cleo	@chouseprofessor	@c_house_jr
Holston	Sarah	@Djsarah37	
Hamilton	Jamie	@Jamie_JeTaime	@Jamie_JeTaime
Grass	Berry	@berry.grass	@thebgrass
Friedman	Mindy	@dappermindy	
Ellison	Joy Michael		@joymellison
Ejikeme	Uzo	@nijashero	
Ebba	Angie	@rebelonpageangie	@AngieEbba
Dunham	Kelli	@kellidunham	@kellidunham
Deutsch	Aaron	@aaronandinsta	
Dane	Penelope G.	@p2theg2thed	
Conner	M. Shelly	@dappervista	@mshellyconner
Comeaux	Claire	@_cowpunk	
Clout	Simonne	@gtacat	
Centrone	Brian	@briancentrone	@briancentrone
Carrigan	Alex		@carriganak
Butler	Jordan	@j0but	
Bergstrom	Elizabeth Hart	@lizhbergstrom	@Liz_Bergstrom
Benzadon	Clayre	@clayrebenz	@ClayreBenz
Baker-Siroty	Hannah	@hannshio	@hannshio
Bachemin	Ruby	@hoopyruby	
Anderson	Weston	@westononsense	
Allender	Lisa	@lisananetteallender	@lisaallender
Abbott	Franklin	@franklin.abbott	

www.ingramcontent.com/pod-product-compliance
Lightning Source LLC
Chambersburg PA
CBHW040402240726
48664CB00013B/1712